MASTER
YOUR CAMERA CONTROLS

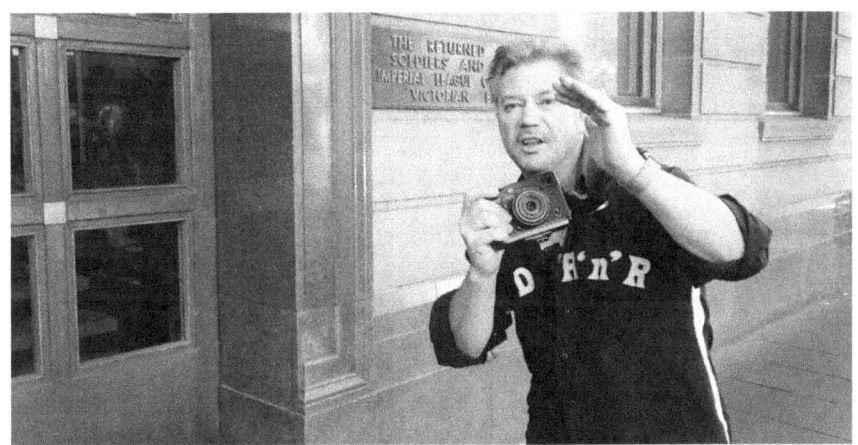

A Practical Fast-Track System to Mastering the
Camera Controls on a Mirrorless or D-SLR Camera

DARREN TILNAK (M.Photog) P.I.P.P

BALBOA.PRESS
A DIVISION OF HAY HOUSE

Balboa Press books may be ordered through booksellers or by contacting:

Balboa Press
A Division of Hay House
1663 Liberty Drive
Bloomington, IN 47403
www.balboapress.com.au
AU TFN: 1 800 844 925 (Toll Free inside Australia)
AU Local: 0283 107 086 (+61 2 8310 7086 from outside Australia)

Print information available on the last page.

ISBN: 978-1-9822-9052-8 (sc)
ISBN: 978-1-9822-9053-5 (e)

Balboa Press rev. date: 05/26/2021

CONTENTS

FOREWORD

A message from the author

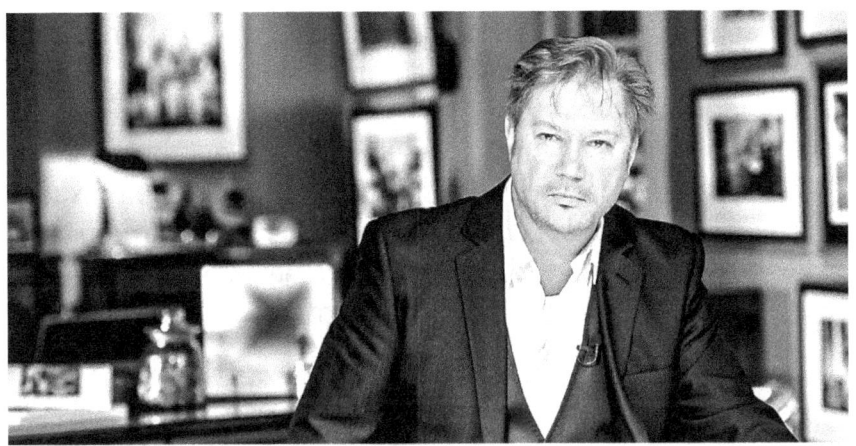

Are you a passionate amateur photographer?

This book was written for passionate people who want to improve their photography. Not just improve it, but grow it fast. You might have heard the adage "A picture is worth a thousand words". Well, it is true if the photo you are taking is well executed. My goal when I wrote this book was to get my friends, clients, students and amateur photographers who want to go pro, to learn photography fast. This book is a blueprint for success if you apply the learnings and also have fun with the exercises. I'm a big believer that when you want to learn something fast, one of the best ways is to use repetition. Zig Ziglar, an accomplished author, motivator and an outstanding speaker says that "repetition is the mother of all learning", and so I use that philosophy to speed up the learning process, to fast track. So how do I do this? By taking out most of the complication with photography, breaking it down and simplifying it, so you have more fun learning at a much faster rate. From a very young age, we learn things by copying and so this book is copycatting a recipe, or formula if you like, that catapulted me to the top of my industry in record time.

What this book is not

It's certainly not the typical science-based book where it is super technical, heavy going and boring. Personally, I always learn faster when I'm having fun, so let's make it fun during your learning process. One very important point that I would like to address is that this book is not designed to go through your camera menu functions. It is to learn the four main camera controls, so you can go out into the world and create exactly what you see. There are going to be a few settings that you need to change on your camera through the menu. If you don't know much about your menu settings there are three ways of learning.

1. Read the manual (my least favourite choice)
2. Google it, or try your best to YouTube it (can be very frustrating)
3. Go back to your retailer and ask for technical assistance

The third option in my experience is the only option and my choice every time.

I'll tell you what this book really is

It's a conversation. I've written this book in a conversational way. Why? It's just the way I teach. I suppose it's because of the mentoring one-on-one with pro photographers and also several national seminars, workshops and so on. The other thing too is that most people learn from a story. So if I share a story with you, I believe you will understand the concepts much better than if I just gave you the A to Z on how you do something. The A to Z my friends, I call "piston mechanics".

So let's do a little visualisation now. Imagine we are at your local café. Over a latte, you ask me how to photograph with your SLR in full manual controls. You asked me this, because we're great friends and because I'm the only professional photographer you know that has a full handle on the science and mechanics of photography. What you are trying to achieve through this catch up over a coffee is to learn how to use your camera, which has cost you serious coin! When you have educated both the professional and amateur alike, there is something pretty special about sitting down with a friend and giving them 30 years experience, but more importantly demystifying the camera controls for the very first time.

Create imagery that is inspiring

Can you see the power once you understand your camera? You now have a license to create imagery that inspires, argues, and educates the viewer about your viewpoint on the particular image you have just created. Personally, it gives me great pleasure creating for my clients, my friends, and my fans. One great thing about what's happening in the world today is the sharing of information, and that's why I feel compelled to share my story, my experience, my 30 years with you so you can fast track and do it much quicker than I ever did. I am not here to sell by comparison, but to just point out the bleeding obvious! There are thousands of books and e-books on photography. I haven't read all of them but the ones I have read, are often written by an author that is a "passionate" amateur photographer who has a learned skill and wants to share it, or milk it for everything its worth. Myself, on the other hand, is simply sharing my journey, my experience and the actions I practice daily as a professional photographer. My budding fellow photographic artist, I wish you an abundance of creativity, fun and sheer satisfaction, while you create imagery that is outstanding, original and more importantly authentic.

The creative imagery in this book will motivate you

The photographs in this book are a culmination of my professional photographs and also images from the public domain. The images are designed to illustrate the message written in the book and also to inspire you.

This book has been produced in black-and-white

This book has been produced in black-and-white. The main reason is that I am a black-and-white specialist and one of the hardest compositional considerations to understand and master is tone. Tonality in a photograph, whether it is in black-and-white or colour, will lead the viewer's eyes straight to the subject if used cleverly. In 2010 I produced a coffee table style photographic book showcasing my imagery called 'My Black-and-White World.' It really illustrates my whole viewpoint and preferred medium when it comes to photography. Particularly portrait work, which is my specialty.

I am not saying that you need to shoot everything in black-and-white. Colour has its place in photography, no question; in fact, it is much easier to draw the viewers' eyes to the subject if it's been shot in colour.

This book has been designed to fast track your learning

This particular photographic learning system has been created in such a way whereby you start at page one and finish at the last page in order. You don't skip the pages or a chapter. Skimming this book is not a fast track way of learning your camera controls. Please start at page one. Do all the exercises in order and I will see you at the end. You'll be glad you did.

Your coach in photography,

Darren Tilnak

CHAPTER 1

So, what's the difference between a good photographer and a great photographer?

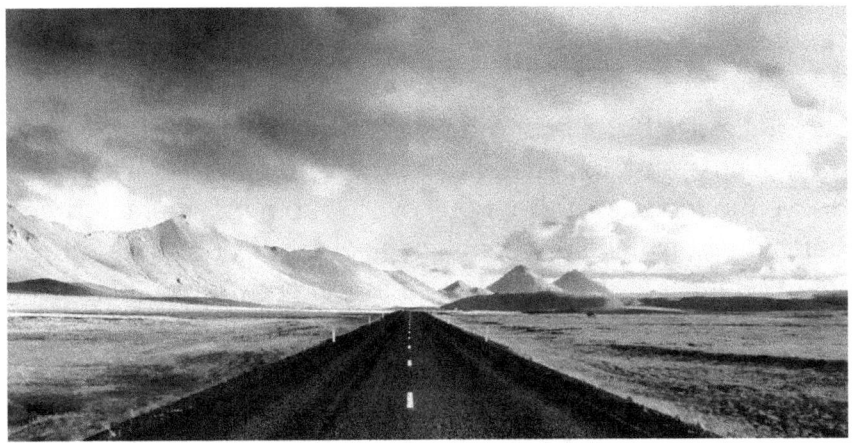

Become the director

It's about being educated, well versed and all-rounded in the area of photography. I don't see the point of a technically well-executed photograph that is boring as hell when it comes to composition and story. The message you will hear over and over again in all my books is that photography is part of the arts. Art is communication, and so I believe your photograph must communicate or convey a message or story to the viewer. So the part and probably the most important part is being a great director. If it is people you are taking photos of, then giving them excellent direction. If it is any other form of image making like landscapes, then you must direct as well. Not the subject but, in this case, yourself. Let me give you a couple of examples of what I mean.

Short Visualisation Exercise

You are driving along in the country and through the windscreen of your car you see some dramatic clouds ahead over the mountains. Now what I want you to do is close your eyes for a moment and visualise this scene.... OK, so you pull over, pull out your camera and record what you see in front of you, dramatic clouds over the mountains. If you are like most amateurs, your camera is on auto settings and the camera has full control over this scene.

Now let's do this scenario again but this time, I am driving in the country, and just ahead of me I see some dramatic clouds above the mountains. So, I pull over, grab my camera bag and before I do anything else I look back at the "cloudscape" above the mountains. Did you notice I have already given this scene a name! Now the very first thing I will do is ask myself what do I want to capture here? Is it the cloudscape itself? Is that the dramatic cloudscape ominously towering over the mountains? Or is it a picture of the mountains with a little bit of cloud creeping into the frame.

What do you want to communicate?

Now can you see that what I'm doing is already asking myself what do we want to capture here? Quickly I decide it's the drama, and the size of the clouds majestically hovering over the mountains that I find sensational. That is the story I want to communicate to my viewer. Now my viewer could be my family, friends, my clients or my Instagram followers. So I grab my camera, take off the standard lens and choose my wide-angle lens. I always shoot with my camera on manual so that I have control over the picture taking. So I decide I want incredible depth, and so I stop down to f/16, increase my ISO to 800, slow the shutter down to get the correct exposure and get ready to take a test capture. Being creative, I choose to underexpose this scene by half a stop so that I can grab the rich colours of greys and reds of the cloudscape. I take the test capture, and the image is slightly overexposed after checking the LCD on the back of the camera, so I stop it down three-quarters of a stop. I take another test shot, check again and, yep perfect. Now that the science side of this capture is handled, the second part of this image making, is how am I going to compose this image to convey my message or story to my viewer? Because, I'm looking for drama and motion I choose to take the picture vertical with three-quarters of the frame filled by the cloudscape and one-quarter of mountains. Click, click.

Understand your camera equipment

Okay did I lose you? If you're like most amateurs, and you said yes that's perfectly alright, and I expected this to happen. Don't worry, it won't take you long to understand what I've made "in camera" exactly and more importantly, how I created this image. We will fast track you. That short journey I took you on just now is the exact way I take pictures and create images that are impactful, stunning and sellable. So in a nutshell, a great photographer is fully integrated and has a full understanding of their camera equipment; firstly, camera controls, then asks themselves "What do I want to say with this image?" They can see "photographically" and then can convey their story or message through clever use of light and strong composition.

Once you complete this book on mastering the camera controls, you will be well on your way to being in the top 10% of amateur photographers around the world.

Know your tools of trade so they will serve you well

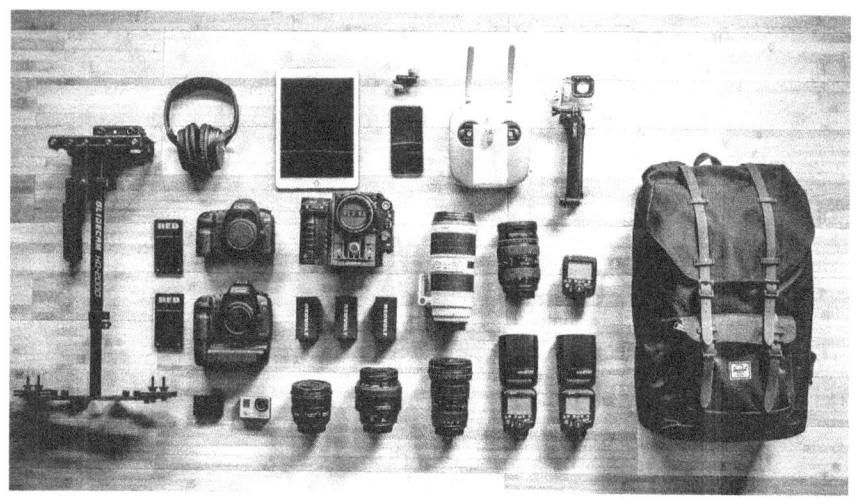

CHAPTER 2

Art versus Craft

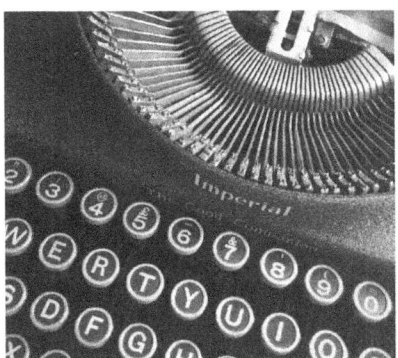 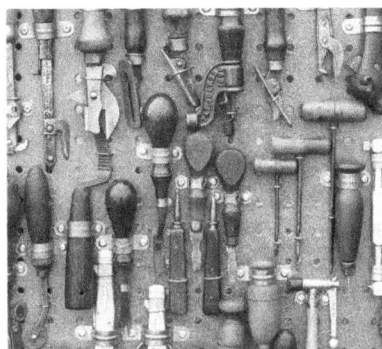

Photography is in two parts.
Art and the Craft

Now that you have my take on what makes a great photographer, and now know that a fully integrated photographer is a great photographer, it's time to dive into this a bit deeper.

Photography is both an art and craft. My experience suggests that very few amateur photographers ever actually learn the science or craft. However, even fewer photographers ever actually learn the art. So let's work out what is craft and what is art.

The definition of ART is... Well, there are several definitions, but the one that jumps out at me and says it all is "Art is Communication".

Okay, let's see if the definition rings true for you. Now photography is part of the arts. It's visual art. Let's explore other areas of the arts.

1. Dance is part of the arts. Ballet is communicating a story, *Yep, that rings true!*

2. Painting is part of the arts. The artist is communicating a story to the viewer.
   That sounds about right!

3. Music is part of the arts. The lyrics and music tell a story to the listener.
   Absolutely, definitely, without a doubt!

I could go on. There is no doubt in my mind that photography is also part of the arts and, "Art is Communication".

Let's move over to the other side of photography. The science or the craft.

The definition of CRAFT is... Again there are lots, but when talking about the science side of photography, the words that stand out for me are dexterity and skill. Other names that jump out at me are "Making, Producing, Fabricating, Tools, Methods". All of these words are the making of the product. The camera controls if you think about it, are the tools. They are the craft of the product. So the way I see it, your camera controls are the "tools".

So if we strip it right down, seeing photographically and having a viewpoint on what you want to say is the art. It's the communication between the author and the viewer. There is an underlying message, tone and transmission to the person viewing the photograph whether it happens to be hanging in a gallery, viewing it online or just looking at it on a device like an iPad or iPhone or Android reproduction.

Understanding the tools and being able to put it on film (or digital memory card) correctly and precisely is the craft. Selecting the right camera control combination, beginning with ISO, then choosing the right aperture, shutter speed and finally selecting the correct focal length lens, is paramount. Above I made a statement, that very few photographers ever really learn the craft and the reason I say this is, they leave the picture taking control to their phone or the SLR or the point-and-shoot camera. They allow the science and technology of their device to make the final decision. It disheartens me to think that people can be so complacent and even though they are passionate about photography have never gone to the effort to learn a few simple fundamentals that will improve their photography, resulting in a lot more understanding and also their enjoyment will go quantum.

Are you different from the rest of the crowd?

I'm very pleased to say that you must be different. Well, aren't you? You must be! So, what brings me to this deduction? You're reading this book. To me, that indicates that you want to be in the top 10% of amateur photographers.

So, I suppose what you need to know is that the camera, when used correctly, becomes an extension of your eyes. However, the only way you'll be able to capture what you see on film is by understanding your camera controls or what I call the "Creative Camera Controls". We now know that photography is split up into two specific areas - Arts and Science. Knowing that, you can concentrate on one particular area, and you can focus like a laser beam, on an individual area of specialisation, which, incidentally is what this book is all about. For amateurs that are passionate about photography and want to take incredible pictures, they first must pay their dues.

Another word for fast-track is copying

This book teaches you all the creative controls of your camera in a clear and concise language, so for the first time, you'll be confident, intelligent and have a full grasp of the craft side of picture taking. Once you've completed this book, I strongly urge you to join me in my video series based on this book. It will be like having one-on-one sessions with a mentor. It's like I'm there with you every step of the way. The video episodes are also aligned with this book so you can take this book with you always, but the amazing thing about the video series is as long as you have an internet connection you can view the set anywhere, anytime and as many times as you want. Imagine, you're travelling on the tube in London.

Join me as I coach you, one-on-one in my video series

You're on your way to work, just like most worker bees in the carriage, but as you look around, everyone in the carriage is reading the paper, probably reading about death and destruction. Conversely, you fire up my video series and want to learn more about how the aperture works. You put on your headphones, transporting you to my studio in Melbourne Australia, where I have a one on one photographic mentoring session with you. You make a few notes, and you don't even need to have the camera in front of you to be in the classroom with me. That's the beauty of my video series. You see, we learn by copying, and so you watch me in the video talking all about how the numbers don't make any sense and how the aperture numbers are very confusing for amateurs. For instance, one of the largest lens apertures is f/2.8. You would think because of the small number the aperture has a little hole. However, it's the opposite and one of the most complex areas of the camera. Unless this is defined, cleared and totally understood this thing called the aperture could be the most frustrating part of taking photos in full manual mode.

Over the last 30 years I've employed more than fifty photographers, and I've seen hundreds of portfolios across my desk, and one thing that stands out, is that most new era digital photographers don't have the correct ABC in photography. It's also an observation that some men and women seem to have a greater understanding when it comes to the science side of photography than others. This also seems to be true when it comes to the art-side of photography also. If you have never been all that good with science this book should be refreshing for you.

You must learn the mechanics first

I suppose the children that played with Lego and did crafty things as they were growing up regardless of gender, will probably get the mechanics of photography much quicker because it's just part of their nature. Conversely if you happened to be a child that used your imagination a lot while you were growing up you'll probably find that the art-side will be much easier for you. Here is one observation when it comes to learning the camera controls or the craft side of photography. When I have conducted a series of seminars or workshops to do with the camera controls, 80% of the attendees are women. I find that statistic quite interesting. They are passionate photographers but have trouble photographing with their camera on manual settings. This book is for everyone that wants to become an outstanding amateur photographer, or also feels compelled to take full control of the decision-making, when photographing a scene, whether it is for love, money or just wanting to feed the inner artist.

Study the images on the following page. What is the author communicating to you? How have they used the "Creative Camera Controls", (their tools) to get their message across to the viewer? When you complete this book, you'll have a greater understanding of why the author chose these compositions and tools.

An urban street scene in Melbourne's CBD. This image is titled "Cafe Legs" Author: Darren Tilnak

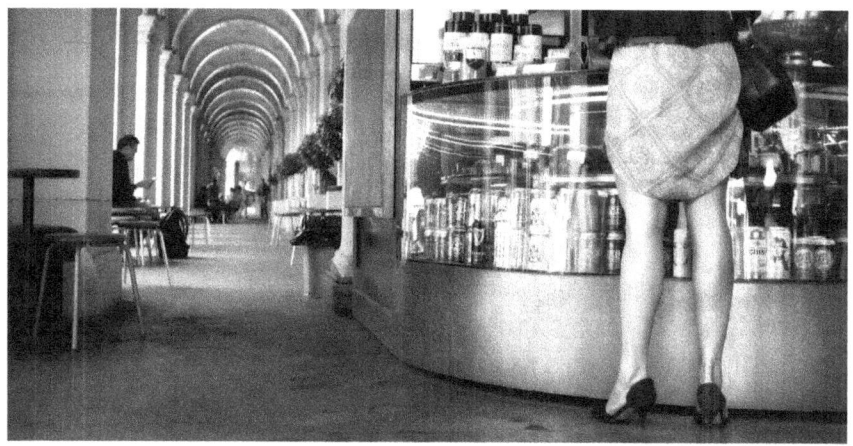

An urban street scene in Melbourne's CBD. This image below is titled "Laneway Interlude" Author: Darren Tilnak

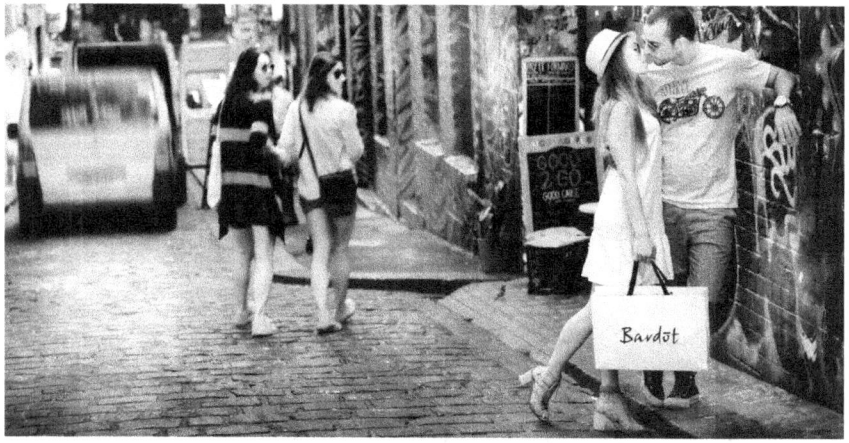

CHAPTER 3

Photographic integration

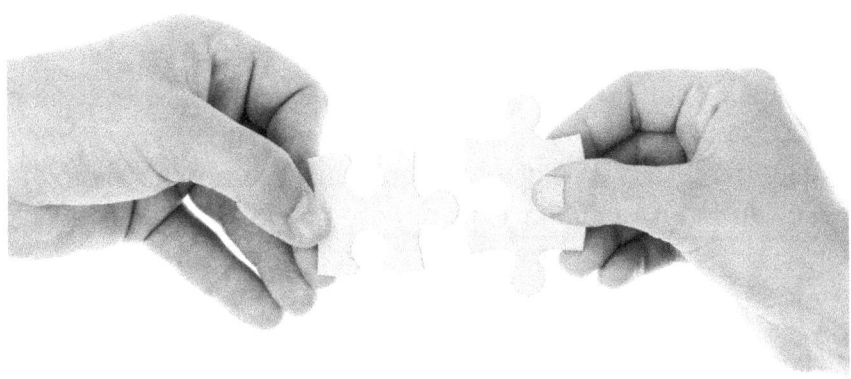

Blending both parts of photography together

Getting back to the definitions of art and craft when you combine them your photography becomes fully integrated. Okay another thing that you will find with me is I am a stickler for definitions. The reason for that is if you can define it or look up the definition you have a greater understanding of the subject matter. So... let us define integration.

◄) **integration**
/ˌɪntɪˈɡreɪʃ(ə)n/

See definitions in:

All   Sociology   Mathematics   Psychology

noun
noun: **integration**; plural noun: **integrations**

1. the action or process of integrating.
    "economic and political integration"

    Similar: combination   amalgamation   incorporation   unification   consolidation   ∨

    - the intermixing of people who were previously segregated.
      "integration is the best hope for both black and white Americans"

2. MATHEMATICS
    the finding of an integral or integrals.
    "integration of an ordinary differential equation"

Integration in photography

Relating to photography, the words that jump out at me in this definition are _fusing, blending, consolidation._ It's like baking a cake. Before you start to add and mix the ingredients, you have to make sure that you've got all the ingredients. You blend and consolidate all of the ingredients to make a winning formula, the winning cake. Okay, so this is how, Fast-track photography speeds up the learning process. I believe that when you start looking at photographic books, stuff on the Internet or YouTube most facilitators make photography very complicated. In fact, I've read books on basic photography that talk about reciprocity failure and light refraction. I mean, we're not going for a bachelor's degree in science now are we? I differ from most authors because my philosophy in photography is simple. I break it down into two parts. Part C (Craft) which is the science side of photography, which is understanding fully, the tools of your trade. The tools being the camera controls of your camera of choice. Part A (Art) is the art side of photography where once you understand the camera controls entirely, you can spend all your time working out what you want to communicate to the viewer. Now this, my friend, is where I spend all my time, directing, composing, creating and enhancing art for my clients.

You must pay your dues

I will take you there, at some point, if you want to go on a journey with me, but not until you have paid your dues. Understanding your camera controls or I call them the creative controls is paramount to becoming a fully integrated image-maker. Let me give you an analogy. To become a world-renowned celebrity chef you have to study all the ingredients and all of the techniques when creating recipes that are mouth-watering and delicious. A top chef understands that the correct balance of ingredients and spices is a craft and is vital for their success.

When I am creating imagery for myself, my clients, my fans or my friends, I am instinctively feeling the camera controls on my D-SLR while I'm taking images and I'm never really looking at the shutter speed or aperture or any other controls. The only thing that I consider looking at is the LCD on the back after taking the first test capture, just to check composition and exposure because the LCD has been calibrated to show correct exposure.

I concentrate on what is in front of me. Stick with me through this book and I guarantee I will fast track you to understanding your creative camera controls in no time, but, more importantly, having fun doing what you love best which is taking photographs of subjects that you enjoy.

Let's move on shall we?

Like a top celebrity chef, you need to know your ingredients intimately. Understanding every part of your camera controls is vital, if you want to create imagery that is outstanding every time.

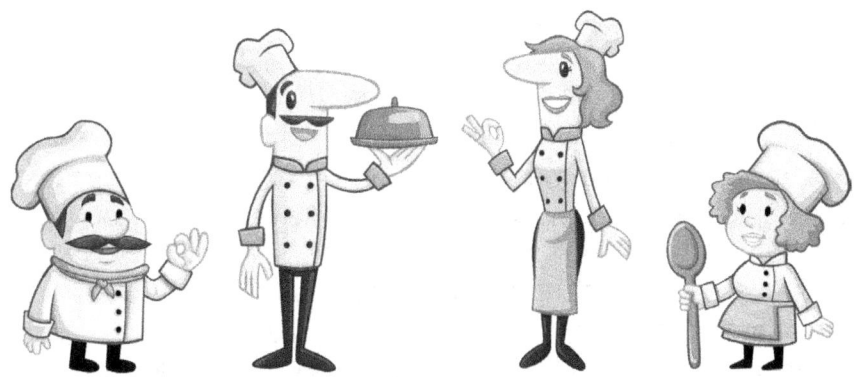

CHAPTER 4

Simplifying the complication

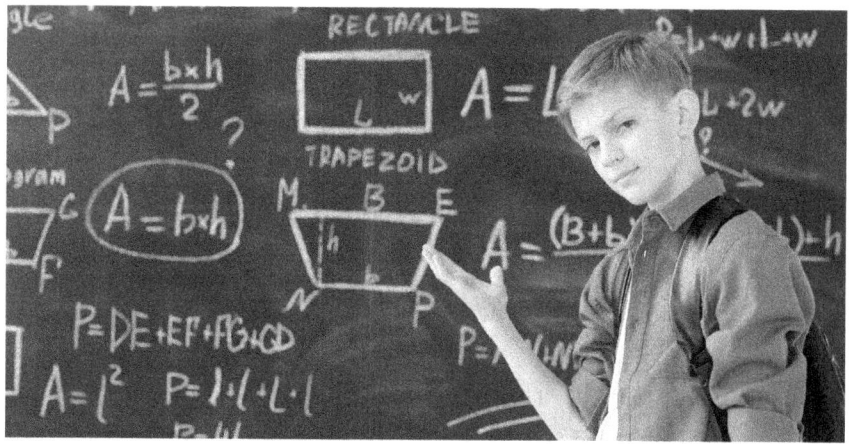

There are a lot of moving parts

As I stated in the forward, I've been a working professional photographer for over thirty years. I have also been a facilitator, coach, and mentor to some business owners in the photographic industry. When they booked me for coaching, there were several reasons. Some photographers needed help with composition, believe it or not, understanding the camera controls, systems, selling and marketing. Time management was a big one also because some photographers made their working life very complicated.

I suppose you're asking yourself what has this got to do with me learning the camera controls? You see, even professional photographers need guidance in all facets of image making. Whether it is in the camera or whether it was post-production in Photoshop. With photography, there are a lot of moving parts and so I believe the best way of tackling complicated situations is stripping it right back down to the bare essentials and building from there.

I was listening to a CD in the car by an American author, who is also a very successful speaker, Zig Ziglar. The disc I was listening to was a live seminar on goal setting among other subjects. And at one point while on stage, he was asked how do you tackle huge goals like for instance writing a book, losing 20 kg, building wealth, etc. In pure Zig Ziglar fashion, he turned to the audience and answered the question with a question, "How do you eat an elephant?" There was silence in the room. He replied, "One bite at a time."

Simplicity is the key to fast tracking.

Have you heard of the "KISS Principle"? Keep It Simple Stupid. I've lived most of my life by that motto, and I found the best way to learn about any complicated subject was to break it down into bite size pieces, also to focus on only one thing at a time. All distraction as we know it just fades into the background, and what's in front of you is crystal clear. I learned my photography in this way. As I mentioned in "Message from the Author", I don't have a university degree. I chose to do short courses on photography, lighting, portraiture and the basic understanding of the workings of a film camera; I am effectively a self-taught photographer.

I've had several spots on television programs, and also various published articles featured in photography and lifestyle magazines and newspapers about my works, awards, etc. When interviewed, one standard question that seems to be asked of me all the time by journalists is, do I have a degree or do I have formal training? I answer that question very confidently with "No I'm a self-taught photographer." The reason for this, I believe is that photography courses are very expensive, time-consuming and complicated. The fact is that you probably only use around 20% of what you learn and apply this on a daily basis, whether you're an amateur or a professional when it comes to photography.

I think you are getting the gist of how I think! I'm not a big fan for learning stuff that you don't want or can't use. Simplicity is the key, yes keeping it simple stupid and learning in bite-size pieces. This book is written this way and my video tutorial episodes are also produced this way.

The universal law of the craft side.

The next chapter we begin the journey of learning the creative controls of your camera. You will notice there is the same application to each control. You'll notice I will dive straight in with very little fluff. We are talking about the craft side of photography now, and so it is more about the "piston mechanics" of the engine, the science, and the facts. So far, I've given you my philosophy about photography, an unabridged version of what I believe. Art is subjective but science not so much. The craft side I'm about to share with you in photography has universal laws. They apply to all camera types and all camera brands. If your camera happens to be a point-and-shoot (which has a fixed short focal length lens and operates in full automatic mode) or you are only using a smartphone this technology doesn't apply.

If you are ready, let's dive straight in and immerse ourselves in learning about this fascinating piece of machinery. This great computer, the digital capture device, commonly known as the digital camera or D-SLR is about to be demystified.

Now the fun of learning begins!

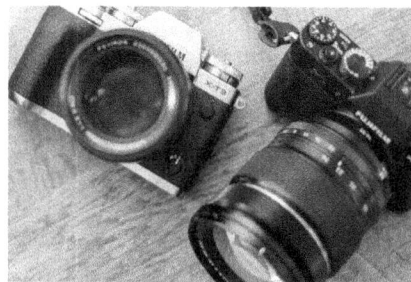 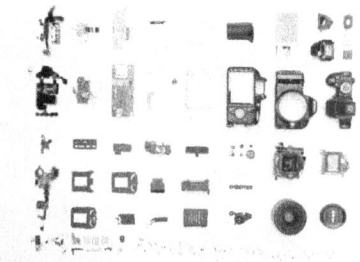

CHAPTER 5

This is how I taught myself photography

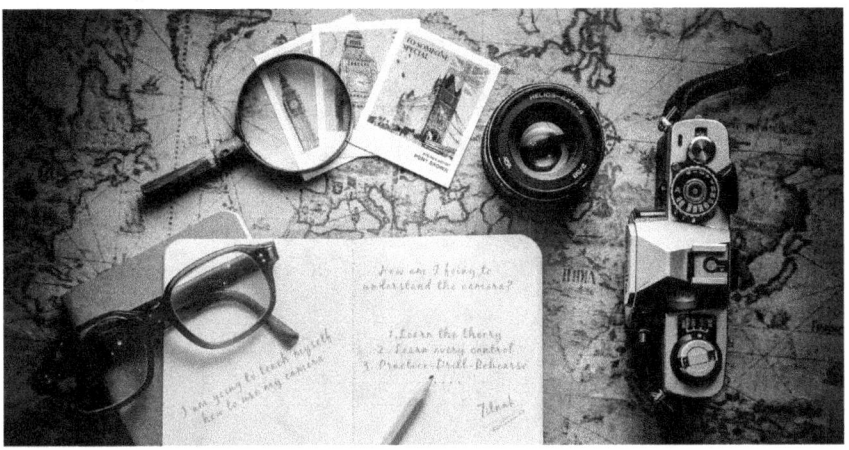

My exact learning process.

This process explained below is the exact process I created for myself to learn the camera controls and photography quickly. I designed this process or learning system back in the late 70's, over 40 years ago.

How did this learning system come about?

Well, I attended a few short courses on basic photography and portraiture, back then. But none of the seminars or courses fulfilled my hunger for learning fast. It seemed like everyone wanted to make photography complicated. A perfect example was in a portraiture course I attended. We were taught to light a portrait with 12 tungsten lights. So as you added another light, you created another shadow, which had to be softened or eliminated, by another light. These days I use one light and a reflector. So back then, I decided to write and establish a self-study course. Just to be clear, this system I created was only for me, not for anyone else. And in a nutshell, the course that I wrote for myself back then, is the foundation of this book, "Mastering the camera controls."

I quickly realised there were four controls I needed to learn, intimately and thoroughly when I looked at my SLR camera. So, they are the four key areas that you and I are going to explore together as well. Why? Because nothing has changed in SLR camera controls, apart from they are now digital, and you can see the image straight away. Just like back then, these are the necessary controls and the four controls are listed in order.

Number one, what film speed or (ISO) do I need to shoot with?

Number two, what shutter speed do I need to choose to capture the image or motion sharply?

Number three, what creative aperture am I going to use to create the real world on film?

Number four, what lens focal length. What lens will I use to convey my story to the viewer convincingly?

An important note here is the first three controls, above are used to expose the film accurately as well, but I don't even think about this as this is just a "given". But we're really covering the camera controls in this book and so for that reason we're only exploring the first three. Which are 1. ISO 2. Shutter 3. Aperture.

1. ISO
2. Shutter
3. Aperture
4. Lens focal length (exposure compensation dial)

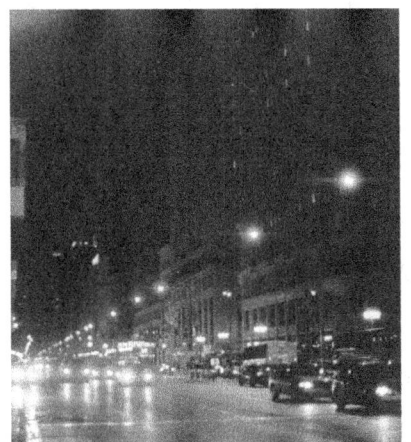
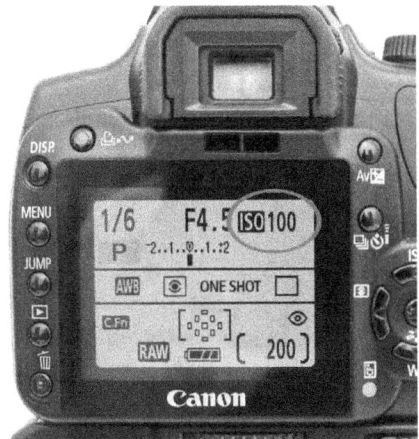
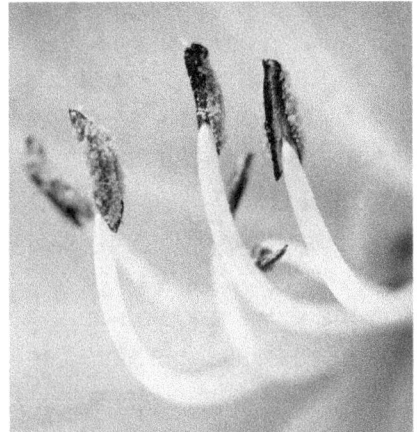
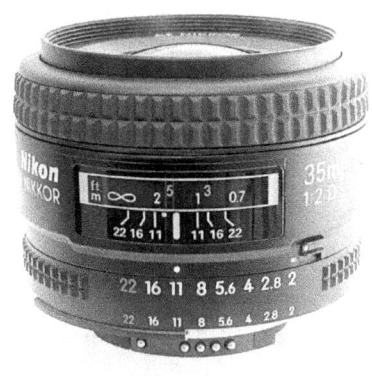
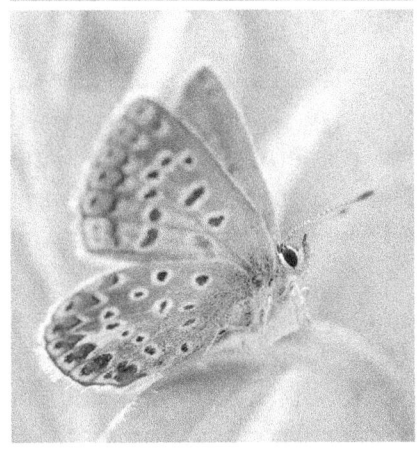
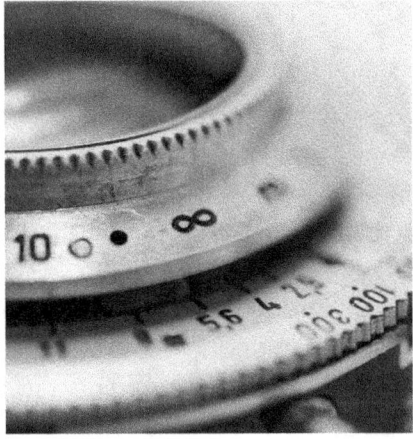

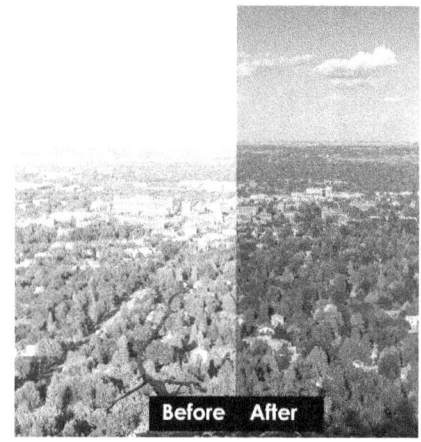
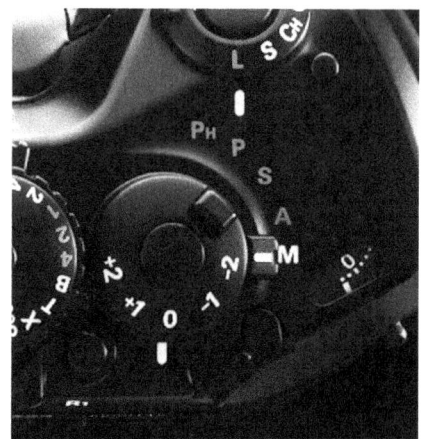

Swapping out lens focal length for exposure compensation dial

I've chosen not to cover lens focal length in this book because effectively it's not a camera control. In fact the choice of lens lives on the art side of photography. I'm suggesting that if you have a mirrorless or D-SLR camera, the learning in this book will apply regardless of the focal length of your lens. Back in my day there was no "exposure compensation dial" and it's a very necessary control particularly when you are on the move and you need to capture something fast. Once these four critical areas have been explored and mastered, you are well on your way to being in the top 10% of amateur photographers around the world.

Like any new learning, there's no free lunch, and so to that end, once we have gone over the theory, I'm going to give you an exercise to do with that particular camera control. I call the exercise, "shoot a roll, learn a creative camera control". I learnt the camera controls intimately and fast this way. This was way back before digital. I also purchased an expensive, nice looking quality book (which became my log book) and a pencil. This is a brief description of how I went about learning my camera controls back then. When I decided to learn about ISO, I bought rolls of film at the time which were 12 exposure film stock. I bought 100 ISO up to 1600 ISO films, to see how they performed and what effect they had. Now I knew all about ISO and film speeds. Of course, now you just dial it in!

Then I learnt each of the controls, and I started off with the shutter. Understanding the shutter speeds and how they work and what effects they had on film. So I adjusted the function mode dial on my camera to (S) Shutter Priority. This feature was the easiest way to be in control of the shutter speeds on the camera, and so for the first time, I was starting to make some decisions when it came to taking pictures.

Learning one camera control at a time

So when I wanted to learn the shutter and how it worked, I grabbed a friend of mine and asked him to ride his bike towards the camera and also across the film plane and proceeded to take photographs. Using fast shutter speeds, like one thousandth of a second and kept the camera on shutter priority. Now, this meant that the camera will choose the aperture being in auto setting and I would just start with a fast shutter speed. Then methodically I worked my way down the dial until I was shooting at around an 8th of a second. I did this twice. Once from a 1000th down to an 8th as he rode towards the camera. Then went up from an 8th to 1000th as he rode across the film plane. A couple of things to note here. I kept the camera on a tripod, so it didn't move. Also back in those days, I only used a manual focus camera. So to get the subject sharp, I also pre-focused on him where I drew a line with chalk on the ground and would then take the shot as he moved over the line. The other thing to note is that after every capture, I would write down in my log book the shutter speed I chose, and the aperture that the camera chose. Once the exercise was completed I had the film developed. I was so anxious to see the results and even though it only took a couple of days to develop, it seemed like an eternity.

Once I got the results back, and the prints were in the order of the shooting sequence, I opened up the log book. Now I was able to see the effect the shutter speed had on each shot that was taken and recorded. So I checked every print and then I could marry that up with the information logged in my book. So in a very short amount of time I did the photo essay learning the camera control, in this case, the shutter speed, on the weekend. Then I would pick up the film that was developed, by say Wednesday and inside a week I had pretty much learnt everything about shutter speeds on my camera. I probably knew more about how the shutter worked, than most, and just by taking one roll, around 36 exposures, doing an exercise to do with the shutter and then logging the information to review at any stage in the future. Then finally, writing my encounter and full learning in my log book as a journal entry. I did the same for the aperture and after that I also borrowed different lenses to see what different results they gave, etc.

The secret system revealed

That's it. That's the secret! That's the system that fast tracked me, to becoming Australia's youngest Master Photographer at the time. It's also the system that is going to fast track you, way beyond the average learning, faster and way less expensive than any formal course and, more importantly, your retention will be between 90% - 100%. The next chapter will inspire, motivate and educate you. So, are you ready to knuckle down and head towards being in the top 10% of amateur photographers?

Okay then, let's begin your learning, with an introduction and overview of the SLR camera controls.

CHAPTER 6

Overview of the camera controls: All modes on the camera and what they mean

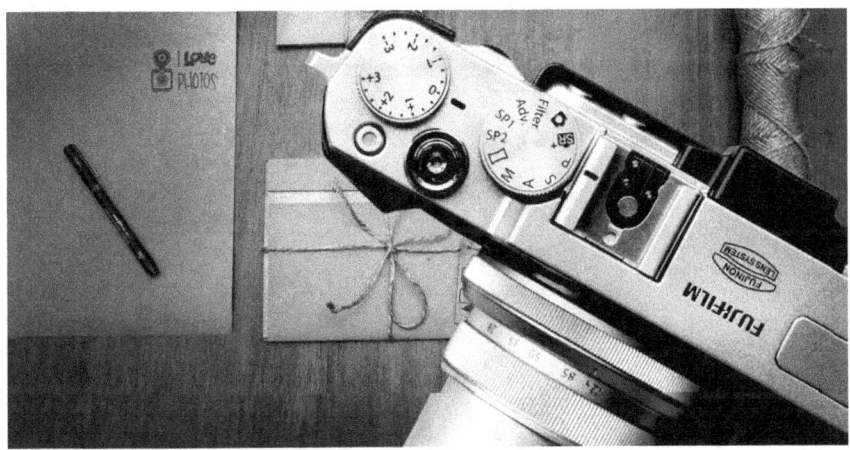

Auto, Program, Shutter Priority, Aperture Priority, Manual

There are five main modes on most SLR cameras and they are AUTO, P, S, A, M. And it really doesn't matter what brand we are talking about here whether it's Nikon, Canon, Sony or any of the other manufacturers of D-SLR cameras, they are virtually the same and universal.

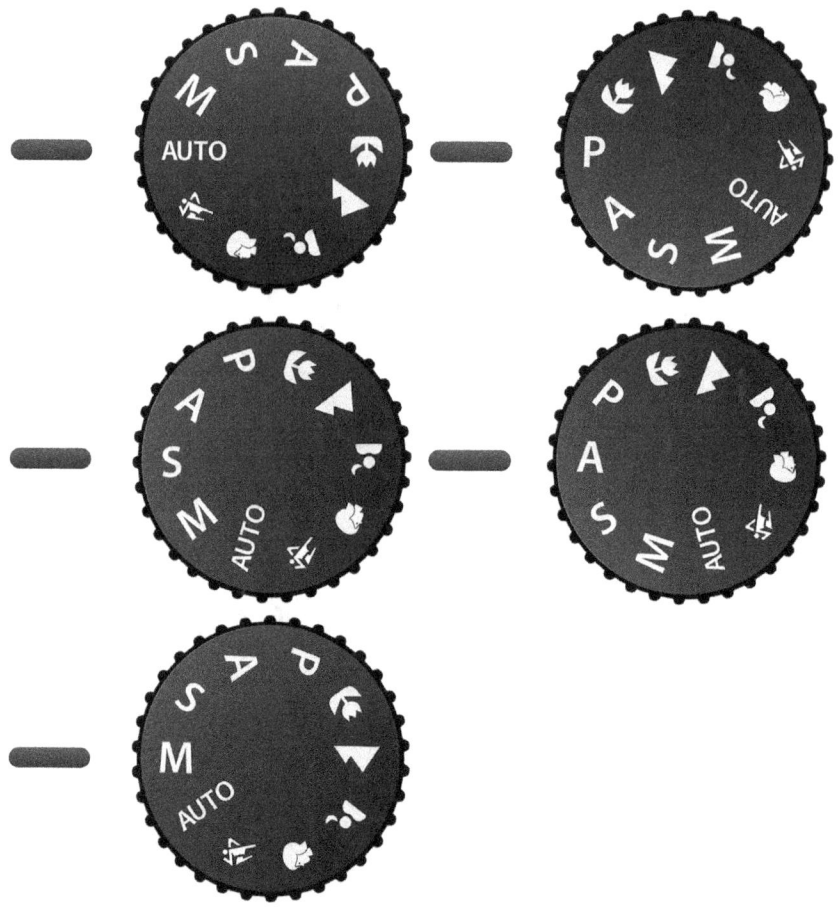

Okay, so the auto mode is probably self-explanatory however, let's still gloss over it anyway. In auto mode, the camera has full control, which means, you don't. Auto mode is full automatic. In this mode the camera chooses everything. ISO, shutter, aperture, and focus. The auto function on your camera even decides whether to pop up the flash or not. Yep, in auto mode, your D-SLR is a very expensive point-and-shoot camera. This is effectively what your iPhone or android phone is doing when it takes a photo. Statistically most amateur photographers when first starting out, or even seasoned amateurs, only use the auto mode and this is why their photography never really becomes ground-breaking. They are allowing the camera to make every decision. It goes without saying that we will not be covering the auto mode for obvious reasons. This mode is my least favourite. Once you have gone through this book the auto mode will become your least favourite as well.

So what do P, S, A, M stand for? P stands for program mode. S stands for shutter priority. A stands for aperture priority, and lastly M stands for manual mode. If you look at most technical books on photography these four modes can be very daunting and we can also spend a week, just on each mode. But I think you realise, I'm here to fast track you and so we're not going to get bogged down with all the science and nitty-gritty, because frankly it's pretty boring. Conversely, what is exciting is the simplicity of each of the modes. So which one of these modes do we explore first?

The easiest and smartest way of doing this now, is to break down each camera control, into singular functions and then apply a simple series of exercises to each of them.

So with your camera in hand and looking at the function mode dial, you'll probably have AUTO, P, S, A, M.

P stands for program

Which is basically automatic settings where the camera is in total control and chooses shutter and aperture for exposure. Now in program mode depending on your camera brand, it also has control over the ISO. (ISO definition will be covered in the next chapter). But still add auto-focus into the mix and you've effectively got a very expensive iPhone that just takes the image or scenery that is in front of you at the time. This particular mode is my second least favourite obviously because you're still allowing the camera to have full control over the picture taking. There is no creativity whatsoever and there are no decisions that you'll be making and for that reason what you'll find is you are reasonably disassociated with the subject matter that's in front of you. That's possibly one of the reasons why most amateur photographers create the same sort of imagery. It's really hard to tell the difference, and generally nearly everything is in focus which means compositionally the image is weak because there's no particular subject matter that your eyes are drawn to.

The only time I would ever use Program mode, would be if I was doing photo journalism, and I am covering a major event, like photographing a celebrity that was walking down the street in Hollywood Boulevard. Or some sort of an accident or disaster where I wanted to capture the essence and emotion of that scene. In these sort of situations, you don't have time to be checking controls or exposure and you are hoping there's something that is either saleable or worth displaying either electronically or in a gallery situation. That would be the only time I would consider putting my D-SLR in Program mode.

So, looking at the function mode dial, there are really only three modes to study here. Because I believe in learning via a gradient, I think we start with the easiest mode first and work our way up to M, manual mode.

What is left on the mode dial is S, A, M.

S stands for shutter priority

So what this means is when you change the mode to S you have control over what shutter speed you want to use when taking the picture. This is the second step to photographing in full manual settings and after the ISO exercise coming up in the next chapter, we are going to get stuck into the shutter. I believe, and treat ISO as a creative camera control. Most books you read on photography consider ISO as part of the exposure only. In this book it is a camera control and the first one we are going to explore. The reason why I want to cover ISO first, is because it is the easiest camera control out of the bunch.

A stands for aperture priority.

So what this means is when you change the mode to A you have control over what aperture you want to use when taking the picture. Apart from exposure, how much depth of field, or lack of, do you want in the image you are creating? Again, you now have decisions to make and are basically in control. This is the 3rd step to photographing in full manual settings and once completed will have a profound effect on your image making. That is for sure!

M stands for manual mode

So what this means is when you change the mode to M you have full control over all your camera controls. My take on this is, M stands for Master. What ISO, what shutter speed and what aperture you want to use when taking this award winning picture. This is the ultimate step to photographing impactful imagery and now you are the Master.

Shooting raw or JPEG

Now at this point, I would like to cover, what type of file type to shoot in. Do you normally shoot in JPEG, or RAW? In my professional working life I only shoot in JPEG. Why? Because my exposure is always within a third of the stop (accurate) and also the file size is reduced dramatically making it much easier to work with and doesn't take up hard drive space like RAW or time downloading and processing like RAW. However, a lot of amateurs that I have mentored have chosen to shoot RAW, because it firstly is more forgiving, similar to what negative film is like. Secondly, it gives them a lot more ability to adjust and manipulate the file. I'm going to leave that up to you, you have the choice in your menu settings and you'll be able to choose the file type and also the quality of the file. I do suggest that you shoot for quality all the time. So if you do choose to shoot JPEG make sure it is in FINE and highest quality file available with your camera. Also, get a fast card reader, at least USB 3 or use thunderbolt if you use Mac.

As I suggested in the forward, if you're unaware of the many settings in the menu of your camera, this book is not about that, and to fast track you in that area, just go back to your retailer where you bought the camera and get them to set the file type for you along with auto-focus etc.

Also in closing, make sure you have purchased a very nice book which will become your photographic log book and a nice pen or pencil and make sure you always have those in your camera bag. In the next chapter there is a short "To Do List" to be completed before we can master the camera controls, so let's get these things sorted so I can fast-track you!

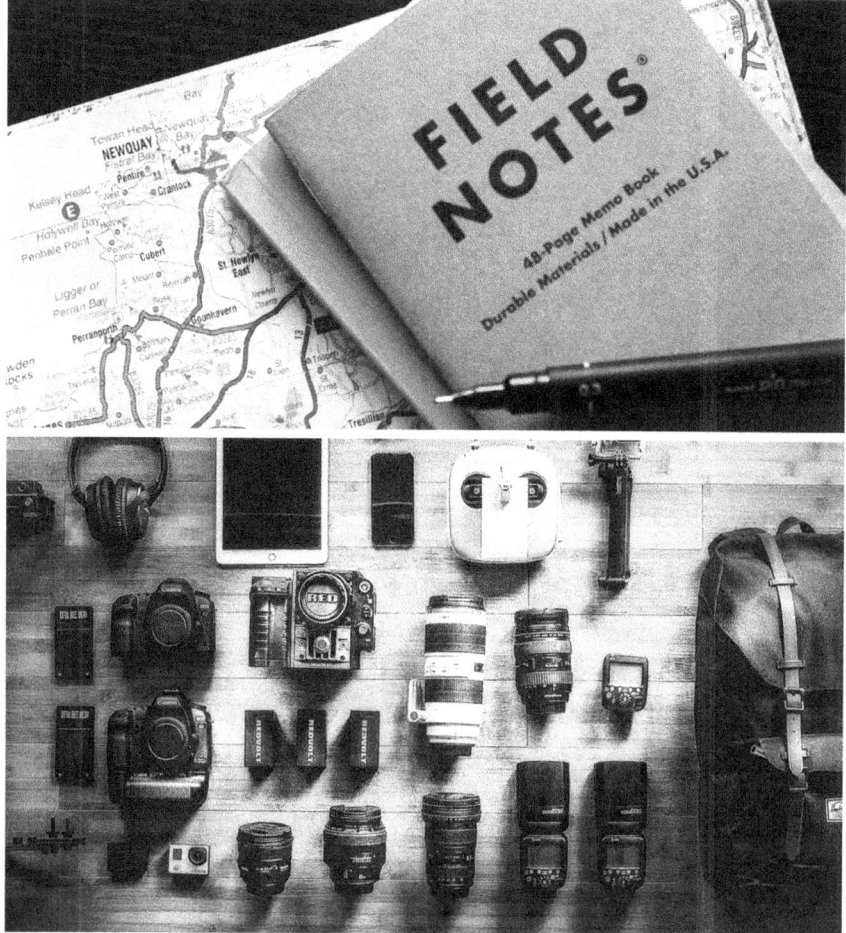

CHAPTER 7

First things first

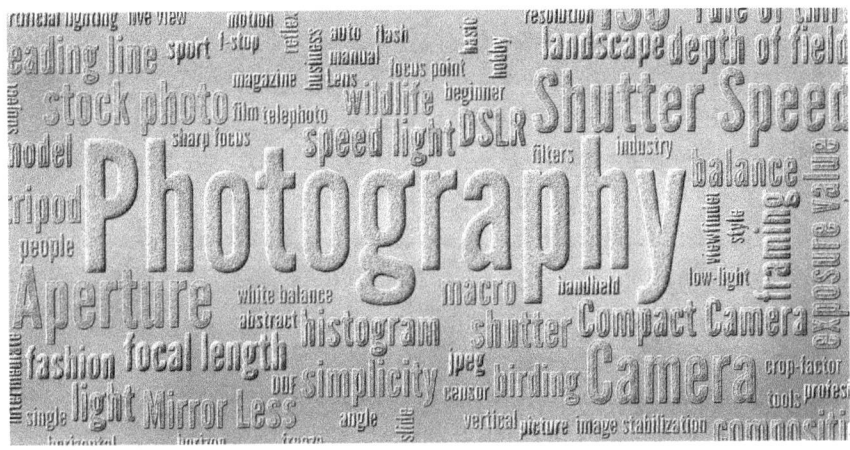

Definitions and photographic jargon

Words mean nothing unless you understand them. Photographic jargon can be confusing and can also bog you down. Time and time again you'll hear me talk about the importance of definitions. With definition comes clarity. You might have read articles or even watched a YouTube video and the facilitator says that they stopped the lens down by one stop. Or the image was one stop over exposed. Or have you ever wondered what the F means in "f-stop" when we start talking about the aperture ring on your lens. So below I would like to just give you a brief definition on a few of the words that are used in the photographic arena.

So I am here to demystify a few words the photographers throw around, like aperture, f-stop, focal length, exposure compensation, etc. Once we explore these words, you'll have a greater understanding, which will mean you'll learn at a much faster rate, which is what we're all about. The photographic jargon that I'll be covering is only the few key areas which will help you master your camera controls and fast track you to be in the top 10% of amateur photographers around the world.

Okay, let's go over the photographic jargon that you'll see and read all the time to do with your mirrorless and D-SLR cameras.

ISO: Stands for: (International Standards Organisation). The definition: the ISO on your D-SLR camera is a control whereby you can change the sensitivity to the light on the CCD or digital sensor. Back in the film days, it used to be called ASA. (American Standards Association) They changed it in the 90s to ISO. In the former days it meant the film speed or again, the sensitivity to light the film had. The higher the ISO, the more sensitive to light. So, if the film was 100 ISO it was less sensitive to light and also had a much finer grain. This was a big choice amongst photographers who were looking for high-quality images that could be enlarged without seeing much grain. As you went up to 1000 ASA or even 1600 the grain became very evident, and so, it was only used when shooting in low light situations or when the photographer wanted to use a lot of grain for specific artful expression.

On your D-SLR camera all you have to do is dial in the ISO or film sensitivity that you want. It certainly makes life easy when you can change it just using a dial. With digital, the film grain is now called noise, which is the digital version of grain. Again it's not necessarily pleasing to the eye for most and particularly if you want to make enlargements for the wall that are sizeable. However, I believe that there are specific applications where noise looks fantastic in photographic art pieces. A perfect example might be shooting a landscape in colour using a lot of noise where it has that real renaissance or impressionist painter feel. The same goes for portrait work. Again the impressionist period where Renoir would paint portraits.

Correct exposure: Correct exposure is a combination of ISO,

Shutter Speed and Aperture. When these three camera controls are chosen accurately the exposure on the digital sensor will be correct. The image, once correctly exposed will offer the highest amount of information and quality so that enlargements can be produced with the highest quality.

Shutter speeds: The shutter on a D-SLR camera, is a blind or curtain that opens and closes at intervals between one second and one 4000th of a second, where light reaches the digital sensor. Choosing the correct shutter speed is vital for correct exposure but it also has another important function, and that is to either create blur in the image or freeze motion.

Aperture: The aperture on D-SLR cameras is perhaps the most misunderstood of all of the camera controls. The aperture is the opening in the D-SLR camera lens, through which light passes to expose the digital sensor. The size of the aperture is adjustable. Aperture size is usually calibrated in f-numbers: the larger the number the smaller the lens opening. The aperture is combined with the shutter to offer correct exposure. But, the aperture's main function is to vary the depth of field. If you choose an aperture size of f/2.8 you'll have a very shallow depth of field (see depth of field for definition). Conversely, if you chose an aperture size of f/16 you'll have a greater depth of field, where everything is sharp from 6 feet to infinity.

F-Stop / Number: The f-stop or f-number indicates a size lens opening on your D SLR lens. The common f-numbers or f-stops are f/1.4, f/2, f/2.8, f/4, f/5.6, f/8, f/11, f/16, f/22. As suggested in the Aperture section the larger the f-number the smaller the lens opening. So in the series above f/1.4 is wide open, meaning it is the largest aperture opening and f/22 is the smallest in the series. The f-stops work in conjunction with the shutter speeds to give accurate exposure settings.

Depth of field: Depth of field is the zone that is in focus at all times.

Depth of field is the distance between the nearest and furthest objects that appear acceptably sharp focus in your photograph. Depth of field depends on the lens opening,(Aperture) the focal length of the lens and also the relative distance from the camera to the subject matter. A perfect example is that you might choose an aperture of f/5.6 and initially you take a full-length photograph of a person. There will be a medium amount of depth of field. Now if you were to bring the camera closer to the subject, where the person now is filling the frame in a half length photograph, you'll notice that the depth of field is now a lot more shallow and everything in the background is a lot more blurry.

Focal length: The focal length is the distance between the digital sensor and the optical centre of the lens when the lens is focused on infinity. Generally the focal length of a lens is measured in millimetres and is generally on the lens mount. What goes hand-in-hand with the focal length is the angle of view. For example, if you have a 300 mm lens you have a very narrow angle of view. Conversely, if you were to put a 35mm wide-angle on your camera you have a wide angle of view.

Zone focusing: Is a very popular technique whereby you choose a long focal length lens like a 200 mm mixed with a wide aperture, which will give you a very shallow depth of field. When this technique is executed properly, the viewer's eyes have to go to the subject that you have focused on, as everything else is out of focus.

Function mode dial: The function mode dial enables you to choose between functions. This was covered in the last chapter there are five main functions or modes. Auto, program, shutter priority, Aperture priority, manual mode.

Auto mode: In auto mode the camera automatically chooses the correct exposure and focus. So effectively the camera controls all functions including popping up the flash if your SLR has flash. Your D-SLR camera becomes a point-and-shoot camera.

Program mode: In program the camera is looking for the correct exposure. The camera chooses both the shutter speed and the aperture automatically. Unlike auto mode, in program it only chooses the two major camera controls. The shutter speeds and the aperture lens opening.

Shutter priority: In shutter priority mode you have the ability to choose the shutter speed that best suits you. The camera then will choose the aperture lens opening to compensate and give the correct exposure. This function mode is when you're wanting to freeze the action in a sporting event or creating motion work to give you the illusion of speed.

Aperture priority: In aperture priority mode you have the ability to choose the aperture lens opening. This mode is preferable when a shallow depth of field is needed or vice versa when shooting landscapes and you want a large depth of field. (This is my second preferred mode, just so you know!)

Exposure compensation dial: The exposure compensation dial is part of every mirrorless camera and also DSLR camera. It effectively changes the exposure very quickly, in generally thirds of the stop. It's a very handy tool if you are photographing on-the-fly, when you are using either aperture priority or shutter priority. You can increase or decrease exposure without having to take your eye away from the viewfinder.

Below is a checklist of tasks or items that are required to fast track you. Some of these settings that you need to change on the camera will be through the menu system.

A. ISO 800
B. Autofocus (fire when focused)
C. Autofocus (Change to tracking, following movement)

D. Change camera mode to M (Manual Mode)

Tools and items required to complete exercises

A. Tripod or monopod
B. A family member or friend to be your model (not for the ISO exercise)
C. Several Flash cards or SD cards
D. Digital card reader
E. Editing software that displays metadata

Just a reminder: Ask your retailer for assistance

As I have already suggested in my forward, a quick trip to your retailer where you purchased the camera will probably be an important trip to get the most out of this book and also video series. Because once you can change a few of the settings in the menu system you are well on your way to knowing, understanding and, more importantly, mastering the camera controls.

The first setting is The ISO, which is (film speed sensitivity).

I would like you to change the setting, so the ISO is 800. Now I am not sure about some other cameras, but with the Nikon, there is a little button at the back of the LCD screen where you can directly change your ISO using the thumb dial. However, this might be different on your camera if it is a Sony, Canon, etc., so refer to your camera manual that came with your camera, or contact your retailer.

The second setting that needs changing is the focus mode. (Menu)

I would like you to put your camera on auto focus. Most manufacturers have four of five different auto focus modes within the menu system. The focus mode that I'm suggesting is "Only fire when in focus". What this means is when you press the shutter, if it's not in focus the camera won't fire. By changing these settings, you immediately will have more confidence when taking pictures because the images will always be sharp which is the very least anyone should expect with this incredible technology these days.

Now's the time to get excited because we are going to study and learn the important creative camera controls, in the next few chapters.

Usage See note at definition.

definite article *n.* the word (*the* in English) preceding a noun and imply a specific instance.

definition /,defɪ'nɪʃ(ə)n/ *n.* **1 a** defin **b** statement of the meaning of a v etc. **2** distinctness in outline, esp. photographic image. [Latin: relat: DEFINE]

definitive /dɪ'fɪnɪtɪv/ *adj.* **1** ((answer, verdict, etc.) decisive, r

CHAPTER 8

ISO: International standards organisation

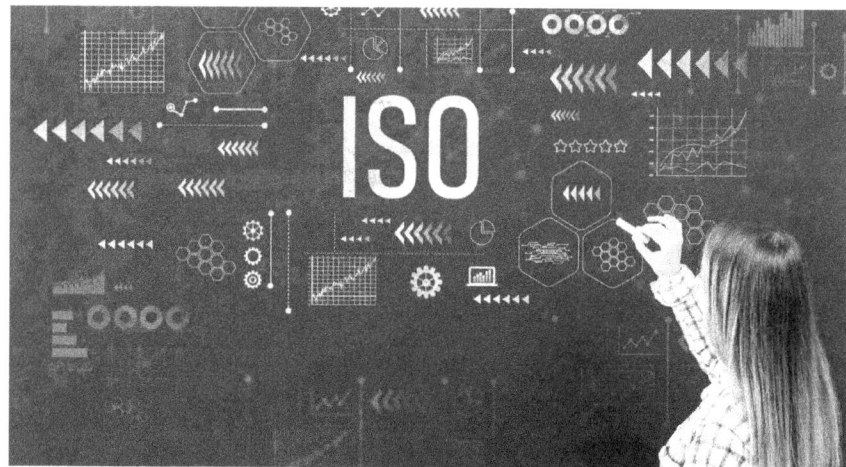

ISO: The easiest of all the camera controls

Now I thought I'd start with the ISO function, why? Well, as I said in the previous chapter, it is the easiest of all the controls to understand and secondly, depending on your lighting situation, will be the first decision that you need to make when you are photographing in full manual mode.

ISO: A full explanation

Okay, so what is ISO? It's the film speed. In a nutshell, it is the sensitivity to light that hits the CCD or digital sensor. The higher the ISO, the more sensitivity to light and the opposite is also correct, the lower the ISO, the digital sensor is less sensitive to light. There is also one other important point that you need to know about ISO and sensitivity. We have established, the higher the ISO, the sensor is more sensitive to light, but also, the more noise or grain will be evident in the picture. The quality of your D-SLR camera coupled with the quality of the lens you are using, will determine how sharp and crisp the image will be. In general terms, if you choose an ISO over 800 there is a good chance that "noise" will creep into the picture. "Noise", or grain, is not recommended when you want to produce quality large images for the wall. In the pre-digital days in photography when we all photographed with film cameras the higher the films rating of ISO the more grain. In the digital world, grain has been substituted for noise. Anything that has a lot of noise is not considered good quality. As an artist and an image-maker, I believe there are creative applications for noise, but that's another conversation.

It won't take you long to see that this creative camera control is an important feature on your camera. Now, when I am out on location, photographing for my client, and depending on the time of day, will determine what ISO I'll dial in.

Your brand of camera determines how you change controls

Your brand of camera will dictate how you go about changing the ISO setting. While I am writing this book, I'm photographing with the Nikon D4, which is pretty much the flagship of the Nikon D-SLR Professional range. To change the ISO on the D4, it's just a matter of holding the little ISO button on the lower back of the camera and using the rear thumb Dial. From there, I can increase or decrease it.

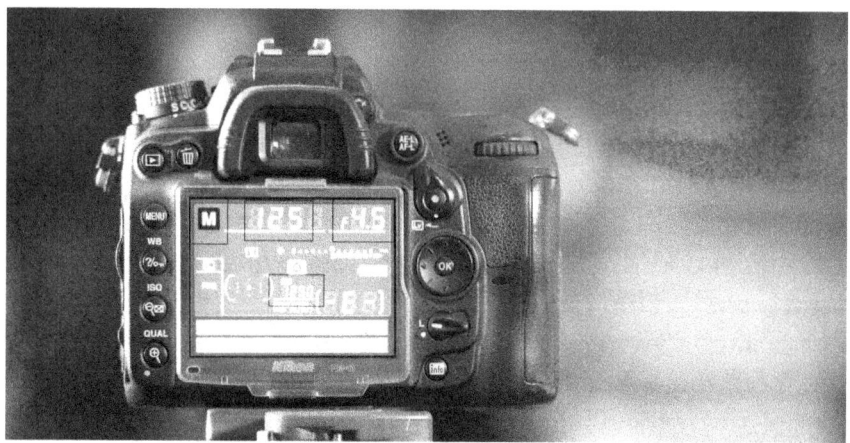

For me as a professional photographer specialising in portrait work, ISO goes hand-in-hand with the shutter speed. Most of my shoots are early morning, and so the quality of light is superb, however generally very low, and so, I need to dial up the ISO on my first and second shoot of the day. You see, if you explore my work online or look at any of my published work most of it is moving pictures. You can check out my work below. Go to:

www.tilnak.com

To make sure the people are sharp and also to stop the action, I'm going to need fast shutter speeds. We will be covering the shutter next after we have done an exercise with the ISO. If the value of light is low early in the morning, or late in the day, the only way of achieving fast shutter speeds is to dial up the ISO to roundabout 1600 to 6400 or even more.

Make sure your ISO has been adjusted

Now in the last chapter, I suggested there were a few housekeeping tasks that you will need to complete. One of them for this very first exercise is going to be changing the ISO to 800. I have chosen 800 because when we move into the shutter priority chapter, I'm going to get you to be photographing moving pictures and you will need that film speed to stop the motion. I hope, at this point, I'm not losing you. Just entrust in the process and I will guide you, and more importantly, fast track you to understanding your camera controls better than most amateur photographers.

I hope you're getting excited because today is the very first exercise. This guided task is probably the most profound yet simple exercise. The reason is you will see dramatic changes before your eyes.

Your logbook is your friend

In the last chapter, I suggested packing your bag with not only the camera, lenses and cards, but also packing another vital tool today, I'm talking about your logbook. In the next chapter, I will lay out a set of exercises for you to execute. The important thing here and the system that I want you to adhere to is after every capture I want you to log the information. Because we're concentrating on ISO at the moment, this will be the main information you should write down. However, I also think it would be a great idea to log what shutter speed and aperture the camera took that photograph with. So even though the ISO, is probably the easiest camera control to understand, I am going to get you also to log information on other controls. That way when we move into the shutter and aperture, you will already have a greater understanding than most amateurs. Like that? Yeah!

As I suggested in my forward "A message from the author" most photographic books on the science side or craft side of photography are confusing, complicated and downright boring. Conversely, going through this first exercise with ISO, and logging the information into your logbook, and for the first time, you should find that there will be clarity. Don't be surprised if you find this fascinating. You don't have to be an engineer to find the workings and controls fascinating as they change to capture the picture perfectly.

Changing your function mode to M for manual

I'm going to ask you to put your camera settings or your camera mode to M, which you already know, is manual. Don't freak out it's only for a short time. The reason is that you will find that ISO becomes just as important, as the shutter, or the aperture and that in full manual mode there can only ever be one setting for exposure, which is accurate. So, just before we begin, please turn your camera on, change the camera function-mode dial to M, change the shutter speed to 500 and change the aperture to f/5.6. Now, I know this might be the very first time that you've set your camera to manual settings. It is just for a short period. But it does get you familiar on how to change all the controls, which you will be using in the future. The next time will be in the second last chapter, and you will be more than ready by then.

It's important to go through this very first exercise to understand one absolute fact. All of the settings and camera controls are integrated. This method is a sure-fire way of fast-tracking you, to understanding each and every control.

Let's get into it.

CHAPTER 9

ISO: A guided exercise in two parts

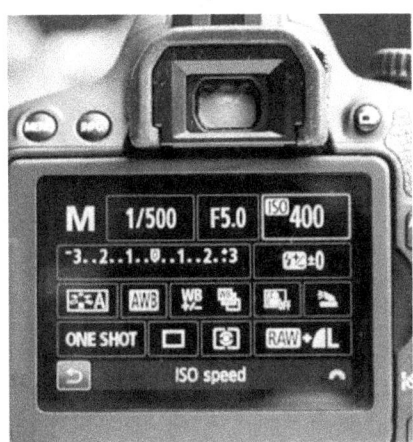 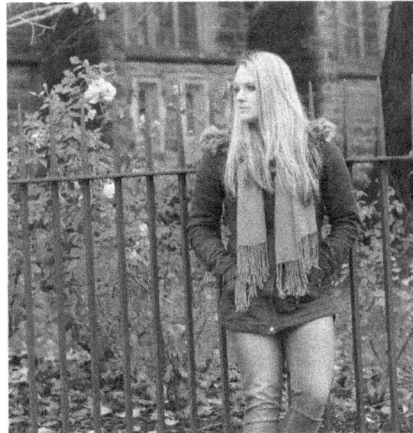

Keep the camera pointing into the same direction

For this very first set of tasks, you don't need anyone to photograph unless there is someone handy that wants to help you out. For the sake of this group of exercises, you only need to be outdoors, and preferably mid-morning or mid afternoon. So you could go into your front yard or backyard to take these pictures. Or just down the street where you live.

I've suggested that you put the camera on M, manual mode. At this point you should have already adjusted the ISO to 800, the shutter is adjusted to 1/500th and the aperture at f/5.6. Now, you can hand-hold the camera for this set of exercises if you want to, but note it is crucial that you are pointing the camera in the same direction and photographing the same subject matter, example a person or a tree or your garden shed. If you're sporting a zoom lens choose a particular focal length and stick to that during this set of exercises. Let's say 50mm. If you happen to have a tripod, it will serve you well at this point, because the camera would be mounted. You can take a picture and then immediately write the information into your logbook. So this first part of the exercise shouldn't take any more than 30 minutes or so to complete ready to download.

Now, just before you capture the first shot, make sure the flash card is formatted, so there is no other information or images on it. You should know already how to format the card.

Journalising your findings

So, if you are ready, let's go and take the first capture with the settings above. ISO 800 shutter speed 1/500th and aperture f/5.6. After taking the first capture if you hit the LCD you'll probably notice exposure is pretty close. Make sure you log the settings into your logbook. The log should be titled "ISO Part One" Capture One. Now I want you to change the ISO to 640 and take a capture. Have a look at the back of the LCD and you will notice the image is slightly darker. Log the settings in your logbook. At this point we're only looking and interested in the camera settings in your logbook. Once you have downloaded the pictures, you can cross reference the images with the settings. Then after that, you can then journalise your findings. This journal entry can be a sentence, a paragraph or a few pages. The journal entry will be the information that will go straight into your subconscious mind and will give you the greatest learning. All the science stuff and numbers won't mean anything at this point, and that is why I'm suggesting journalising your findings. A simple journal entry might be "Wow, what I noticed was that as I increased the ISO and then took a shot it got lighter and got more grainy".

Okay, back to the task at hand. I would like you to change

constantly the ISO dial from 640, down to as far as your camera can do which will probably be around 100 ISO. At some point (ISO setting) the image on the LCD screen will be jet black. Which means there is no information recorded, however, keep going down as far as your camera allows. Once you've completed that, go back up to ISO 800 and start there, and take another capture. This time, I want you to go in the other direction change the ISO from 800 to 1000, 1250, 1600, etc. Continually change the ISO and take a capture for as long as your camera is capable. It might be a roundabout ISO 8000 or 16000. Without getting too deep or too confusing at this point, I would like to make one note. We started the ISO at the beginning of the day at 800. When you change the ISO to 1600, it is exactly one stop difference or double the sensitivity. At this point, what I would like you to notice or take note of, is that the ISO and the shutter work in similar ways. Double the number equals one stop. Half the number equals one stop. So when we move into working with the shutter next chapter, you'll notice the same thing. As you double the number, you decrease the sensitivity by half and visa-versa.

Now that you have logged the information into your logbook and as you look at the back of the LCD, anything past 1600 ISO, you'll notice that you're losing the detail in the image. As you continually change the ISO up to 2000, and right up to 8000 or higher, the image just becomes white noise. In the good old film days, this was called "over-exposed". In fact, even at 1600 you'll find the image is very light (over-exposed) and once you download this picture and import it into your photo editor, some of the information will be lost altogether. Another thing to note here is that digital is not forgiving. This is part of the reason I felt compelled to write this book. Being accurate with your camera controls is paramount, in creating quality imagery for pleasure or profit.

Moving on, I would like to introduce part two of the ISO exercise and a new profound learning experience.

Understanding ISO (Part Two)

This is the second part of the ISO exercises for today. So in the first part, we kept all the other controls constant and only changed the ISO. It meant at the end of the day that there was only one setting during an exercise where the image was exposed accurately. Now in the second part, I would like you to change the camera settings, as below.

Firstly change the camera function mode from "M" to "P" (which is for program).

Now change the ISO to 4000.

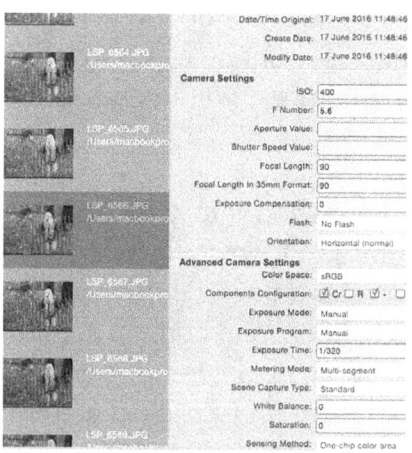 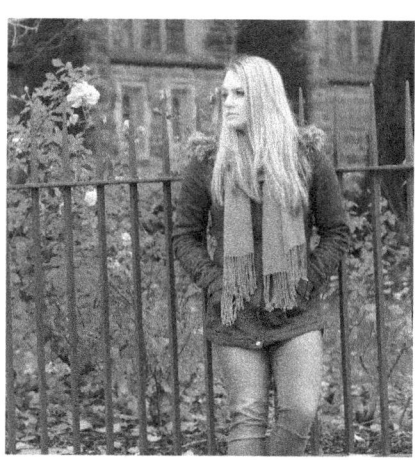

Now in these examples it is very obvious to see that the first image is exposed correctly and within 1/3 of a stop. The ISO is rated at 400. In the second image we have then reduced the ISO to 100 which is two full stops.

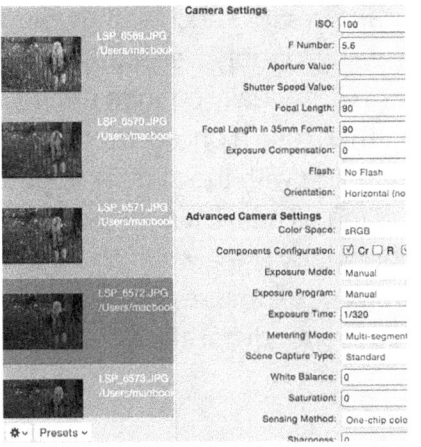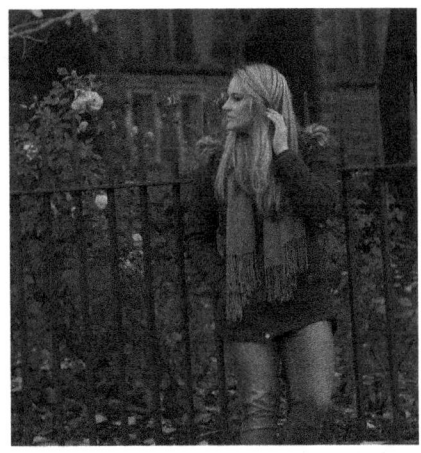

In the third example, we dialled up the ISO to 6400. There is hardly any information left to recognise the subject. This exercise is a fabulous way of understanding how ISO is an important camera control and differing lighting conditions, will determine how often you use it.

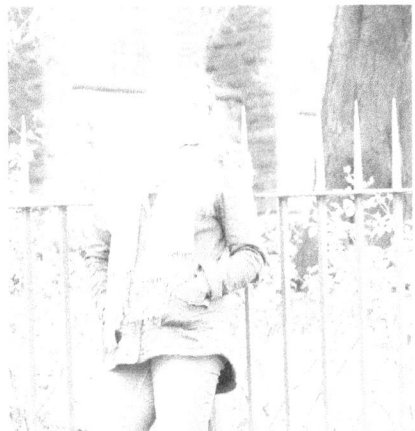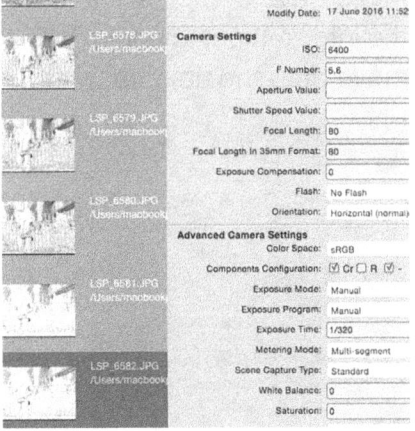

Formalising part two

Make sure that you are pointing the camera at the subject, exactly as in the first part of this exercise. Take the first capture, now look at the back of the LCD. What you should notice is, that the image exposure will be pretty good. Log the information in

"ISO Part Two" capture one. Now take the ISO and start moving it to the next lowest number that will probably be 3200, make another capture, log the information. Continually change the ISO sensitivity by one number less, and then take a photo, record the results. Did you notice what is happening with the shutter speed and aperture? It is important here to log all camera controls (ISO, shutter speed and aperture), and how they are always changing to compensate and give you the correct exposure. Once you've completed this set of exercises, you are ready for the download, which is the fun stuff now.

Time to write in your journal. This exercise should have given you an "ah ha" moment. You know, where the light bulb goes off in your head! Now you should see how the camera controls work. But, this is not the only thing I would like you to journalise. I would like you to write down all of your findings, your observations, and experience, right now.

If you have completed this set of exercises, along with logging the information, and journalising the experience you are ready to move onto the next chapter.

CHAPTER 10

Shutter priority knowledge and understanding

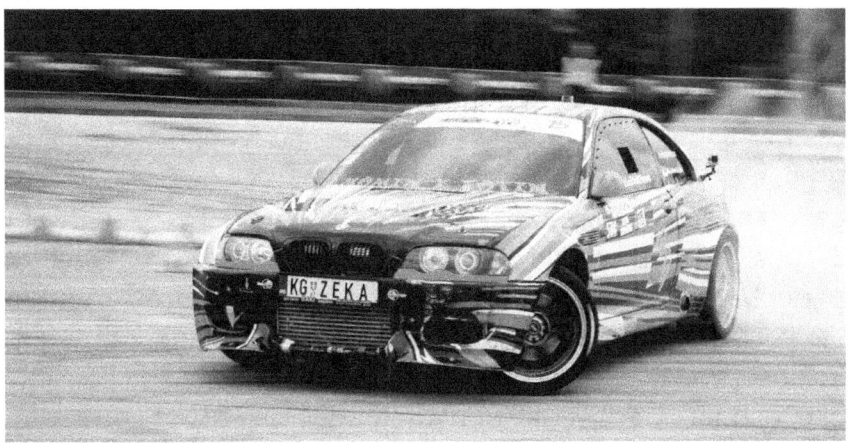

So what does Shutter Priority mean exactly?

It means that when you change the mode to S, you have control over what shutter speed you want to use when taking the picture. The great thing about this is your D-SLR will adjust the aperture to achieve the correct exposure.

The great thing about shutter priority is you are well on your way to shooting in full manual mode. Also, it gives you, the photographer, the ability to make decisions to stop the motion or to create it in your photograph.

Housekeeping before we start this photo essay.

Change Camera ISO to 1600.

Here's your to-do list.

Pack your logbook and pencil.

Pack your camera and lenses, flash cards or SD cards and a monopod or tripod.

Call a family member or a friend to be your model for the day. This photo essay is going to need a model to go through the motions with you, today.

Choosing good light builds confidence

Now, like any good surfer, the type of day you choose weather wise, is important. For the sake of this and all photo essays or exercises, I'm suggesting that you choose cloudy or overcast days. If you happen to be reading this in the UK or parts of Europe where some days are bleak and grey, this really is the perfect lighting situation to start your journey to become a top amateur photographer. Reason, soft light, it's all about the light. You see, you want to get as much detail on film as you possibly can, and an overcast day or photographing in shadowed areas, is how you are going to get that. I am not suggesting going out and shooting in full sun, as it becomes very contrasty, and it is already setting you up for disappointment. Many amateurs photograph in full sun, in the middle of the day, which is the worst lighting situation.

By looking at lighting conditions and picking the light, I am gently getting you to delve into the art side of photography. That's the area that I play in, on a daily basis. In fact, it's the only decision I make consciously, in my career on a daily basis. Light and composition. Now this is truly delving in the art-side and already I'm getting you to step over to that side of photography. So if you remember in chapter one, "My definition of a great photographer", I talk about being fully integrated. Firstly understanding the camera controls inside out, upside down and then focusing on the art-side.

Talking about the "Art-Side".

Look out for my new book.

Mastering the 7 keys to composition

You might have heard the adage "if life is worth living, it's worth recording". So remember to log every capture from this shoot, and when completed, I would like you to write a journal entry. Remember, the journal entry can be a sentence, a paragraph or even a page. The concept here is to get you to write down how you found the process, and if you have more clarity about your image making today. What you'll find is you become empowered because all of a sudden, the lightbulb comes on. The penny drops and probably for the first time you start to understand and demystify the science of photography and the creative camera control, the shutter.

Okay, let's go out with your model, camera equipment and props if you have any, like a bicycle, etc. This day is going to change your photography world forever.

Good luck my friend, enjoy!

CHAPTER 11

Shutter priority: A set of guided exercises

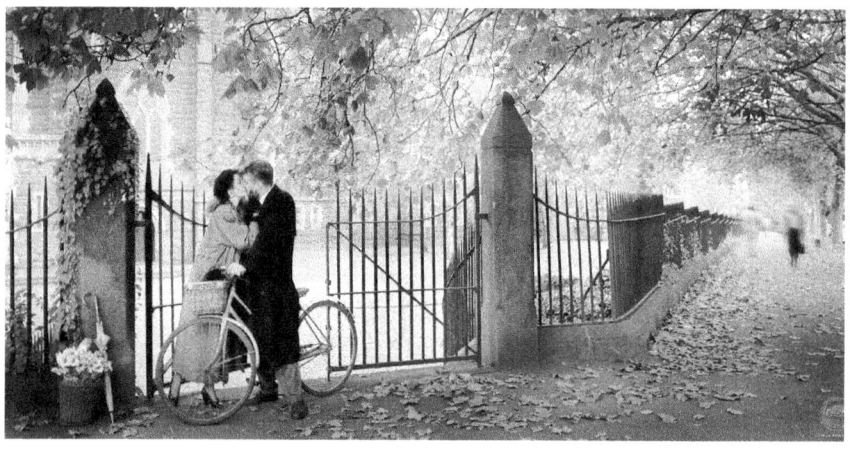

Learning shutter priority the fast track way

Once you are "On Location", and organised, move the function mode dial to "S" for Shutter Priority. Then make sure the ISO has been adjusted to at least 800, though, I suggest bumping it up to 1600 if it is a heavily overcast day. This way you will be able to utilise fast shutter speeds also.

Shooting in Shutter priority is the first step to photographing in full manual settings. Now that we have explored ISO, this is where real creativity starts. The reason I'm getting you to explore the shutter second is because it is the second easiest camera control out of the bunch. So the exercise I'm going to give you at the end of this explanation is learning how to use the shutter for exposure but also to create and stop motion.

You see, I use the camera shutter in my working life for two reasons. Not just to get the correct exposure, but to stop the action as well. In most of my work, I create moving pictures and so, I have to use faster shutter speeds, to freeze the action and to make sure there is no camera movement or subject blur.

Now that you have adjusted the camera controls, shutter speed set to 1/1000 and the ISO on 1600, make a note of what the camera is choosing for aperture.

I would like you to set the auto-focus dial to "continuous" which will track the person moving towards you and keep them sharp throughout this series of captures taken. With either, your family member, friend or partner, and if you're lucky enough to own a bicycle I would like you to get them to either ride, run or walk directly towards the camera.

Shoot a tracking scene towards the camera

Take a series of shots and there's your first scene. Shoot a burst of 8-10 captures. Log the information and then change the shutter speed to 500, again take note what the aperture is doing. Notice that the f-stop number is higher than the last burst of captures. Now, again shoot the series of captures and log the information. Now change the shutter speed to 250 and take note of what the aperture is doing. I'd like you to continue this process until the shutter speed is down to around 4 or 2 which is a quarter or half a second. I would like you to complete this process of exercises while you have the subject moving towards the film plane. Mark a spot from which they will start walking, running or riding. After the burst of captures, ask them to go back to the starting point.

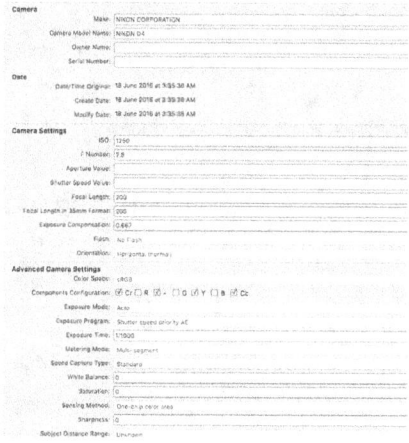
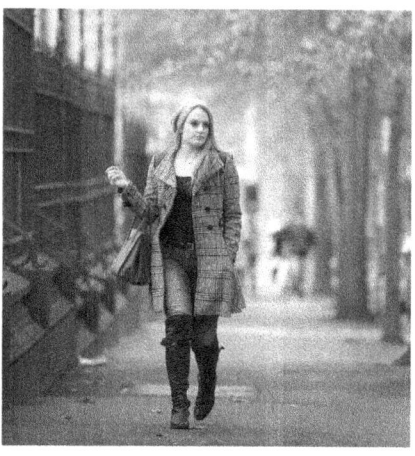

1/1000th of a second is more than enough to keep the subject sharp.

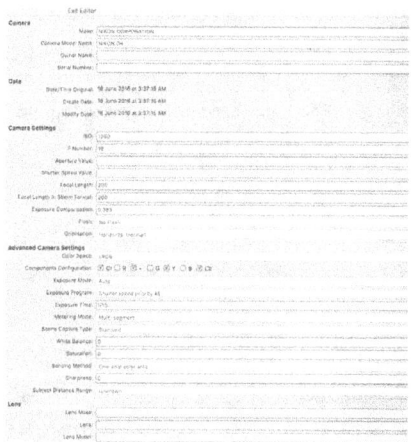
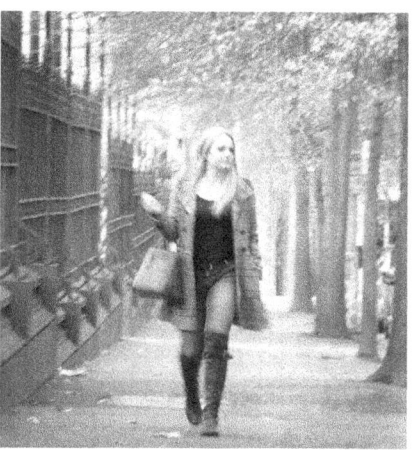

1/15th of a second introduces subject blur and camera shake.

You might notice that the top image is slightly dark. (Underexposed)

The reason for that is even though I compensated slightly for the exposure, the background was very light and the camera's exposure meter didn't take that into consideration. I wanted to show you this, because we're going to be exploring the "exposure compensation dial" in the chapter after the aperture, for this exact reason. This is why I wanted to include this very important and creative control.

Across the camera film plane

The second set of exercises will give you a much greater understanding of how the shutter works when subjects are moving across the camera. What I mean by that, is that they are riding running or walking from left to right. So while the camera stays static, they enter into the image viewfinder from the left hand side and exit on the right hand side, while you take the photographs.

So this time, what you're doing is starting with a slow shutter speed. In fact, let's start where we left off at half a second, (1/2) increasing the shutter speed with every new series of captures. After every new series of photos, log the information and also take note of what the aperture is doing.

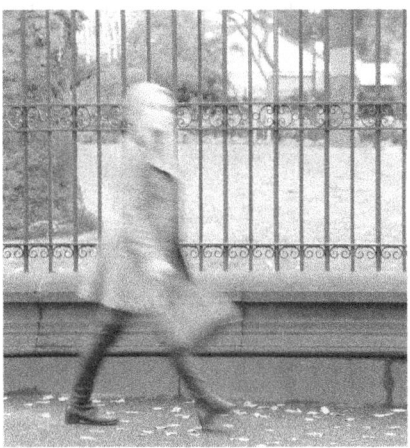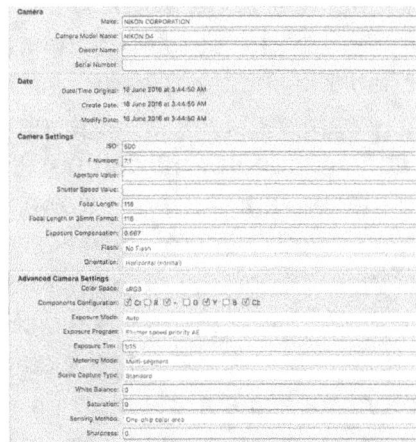

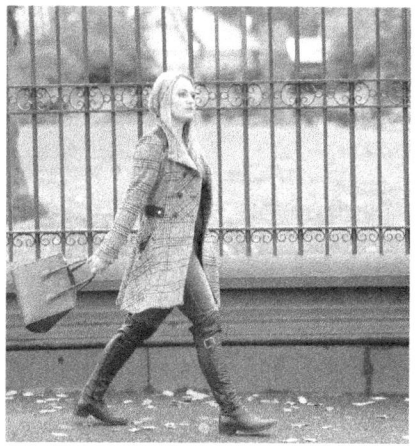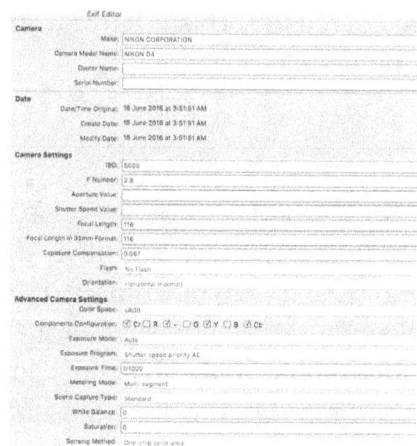

Substantial difference between the top image1/15ᵗʰ and bottom 1/1000ᵗʰ

Camera movement throughout the image

Now while we're doing this set of exercises understanding the shutter and knowing full well it's all about learning how to create motion and also stop action. There is a critical aspect when choosing shutter speeds, and this is when you are hand holding the camera. The average amateur photographer around the world handholds the camera 90% of the time. So it makes sense to understand how the slowest shutter speed you can choose before you get camera shake or camera movement in the image. Notice the top image is quite blurry. I chose a shutter speed of 1/15 of a second. This is exactly the same shutter speed as the image walking towards the camera, however, look at how much more movement there is. As you do this exercise and log the information you will find the results very interesting.

This data is valuable information for all your future shoots

Now here is where it gets fascinating. As you start to log your captures what you'll notice is, with every new scene taken, when you reduce the shutter speed, the aperture changes at the same time. As stated before, shutter speed and aperture are integrated. Now the aperture changes with the number increasing from say, f/2.8 to f/3.5 or f/4. So the great thing about this is your camera is teaching you the camera controls. So for the sake of the exercise, the very first shutter speed you choose is 1/1000 and let's say that the camera chooses an aperture of f/2.8. The next scene you choose with a shutter speed of 500 the camera now selects an aperture of f/4 and so on. Can you see how there is a pattern emerging? As you reduce the shutter speed, the aperture number goes up (reduces the size of the opening). So the camera is now, teaching you exposure. So to correctly expose the film as you decrease or increase the shutter the aperture must increase or decrease accordingly.

As Sir Isaac Newton said, *"With every action there is an equal and opposite reaction."* Let's not forget that there were two exercises displayed today to understand. Firstly for correct exposure and secondly creating motion or stopping movement. The reason I have asked you to bring a model along is so you know how the shutter works in stopping action and what shutter speed does to stop the motion. Once you download the captures, the idea is to be like a detective and see if you can notice any subtle differences in the images when it comes to motion or blur, etc.

Please write a journal entry with your findings. Record everything you notice, no matter how slight. Once that's been completed, it is time to move on to the most misunderstood camera control of all, the aperture. I'll see you in the next chapter, where your photography is about to go quantum.

CHAPTER 12

Aperture priority: Pre-exercise and photo essay

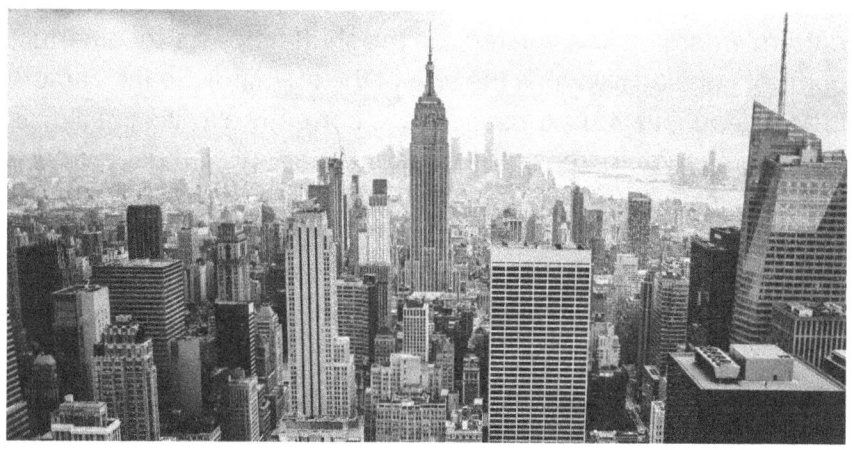

Demystifying the most misunderstood camera control

Here it is, the most misunderstood and perplexing camera control, the aperture. Any grey matter in your mind that you've had in the past about this creative control is going to be smashed. Often you'll find in books and on websites, the author gets you diving straight into the aperture, but it ends up confusing most amateurs because it's complicated in structure. This part of the camera controls is the purest science side of photography. But, have no fear, or concern. I'm here to fast track you, so you're going to love the aperture and how to use this camera control to create incredible, impactful images that are going to wow the viewer.

I am often asked by amateurs what does the "F" in f-stop mean. You already know that I am a big fan of definitions, and when you can define a word or anything for that matter, you get clarity on that subject. The "F" in f-stop means "fractional stop". Now the word "f-stop" is used for both the shutter and aperture. However in my career spanning over 35 years, it has mostly been used when talking about the aperture. When we are strictly talking about exposure and wanting to either let in more or less light to the sensor, we speak in increments of "stops". One "stop" is exactly double the light coming into the sensor or exactly half the light hitting the sensor.

Just before we head out for the day and do our photo essay exercises, I would like to go over these numbers one more time, and I also want you to have a look at the (picture opposite) which represents the size of the aperture (hole) and the corresponding number.

Practice it until you can't get it wrong

The bigger the hole, the smaller the f-number. I'll repeat that. The larger the hole, the smaller the f-number. At this point, a repetitive process is in order. In an earlier chapter, I talk about one of the best ways of learning is by copying. Another fantastic way of learning is by employing a repetitive process. Just do the same thing over and over until it becomes second nature. I remember saying to my daughter one time when she was practising her team Pom routine, "Keep practising until you get it right." And she said no dad, "I'm gonna practice this until I can't get it wrong." Do you like that? Don't practice it until you get it right, practice it till you can't get it wrong.

So, let's do this repetitive process together. Now let's also replace the word "hole" with the word "aperture". With the aperture, the larger the aperture, the smaller the f-number. The smaller the aperture, the larger the f-number. Again, with the aperture, the larger the aperture, the smaller the f-number. The smaller the aperture, the larger the f-number. One more time. With the aperture, the larger the aperture, the smaller the f-number, the smaller the aperture, the larger the f-number. Now, we know that a picture is worth a 1000 words, so let's look at the infographic on the opposite page. Notice that the aperture opening at the bottom right is the largest and has the smallest number conversely, the top left hole is so small, yet has the largest number.

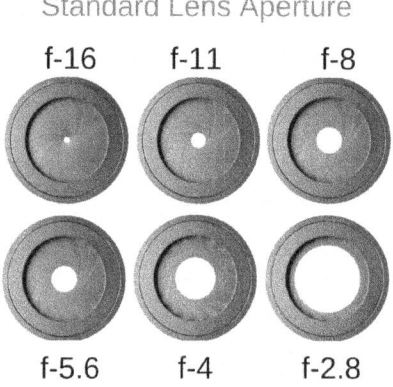

Standard Lens Aperture

f-16   f-11   f-8

f-5.6   f-4   f-2.8

NB: The larger the "f" number the smaller the Aperture

Boom, there you go. The theory session is over. Surely you have a greater understanding of the size of the aperture and the corresponding number now, so let's talk about how to use the aperture on a daily basis. This particular tool or creative camera control is essential to creating a strong composition. No, I'm not going to start talking about the art side. However, the aperture will be the most widely used camera control I guarantee you!

The two primary reasons you'll choose a particular aperture are.

1. Balance exposure
2. Depth of field

Photographing exactly how your eyes see the world

One of the main goals, when you see a scene in front of you, is you want to record it exactly how you see it. But most phones and point and shoot cameras control the way the scene is recorded, and it is often nothing like the way your eyes see the scene. Let's look at what I mean. Look up and I would like you to fix your eyes on something. Stare at it and don't move your eyes away. Now, using your peripheral vision, you will notice that everything, in front of that spot and everything, behind that spot, is "out of focus". That's how we see the real world. To capture the real world, as we see it we need to be opening up the lens aperture in the same way as your eyes. This opening or aperture will be around f/4 or f/2.8 or wider if your lens allows.

Now in this session, you're going to be putting your camera mode onto aperture priority. And in this photo essay set of exercises, the idea is not to spend a lot of time understanding Number 1, balancing exposure and the reason for this is that your camera is taking care of that.

The aperture controls depth of field

The greatest learning here is knowing how to use a wide aperture to pick out one particular subject matter from the background which will make everything else blurred. Or conversely, by using a small aperture keeping pretty much everything in the picture all the way through sharp.

As you go through these exercises you will start with the smallest aperture first. Let's start on f/16 and work our way down to f/2.8 or if you're lucky enough to have a lens that has f/2 or even f/1.4 we will go that far. So I want to take you to what is known as "wide open". It means that the aperture is at its maximum opening. Example f/2.8, f/2 or f/1.4.

So to give you an example I have been shooting with a Leica for many years and I have a 50 mm Noctilux f/1 lens which is nearly the fastest lens you can buy. Now I'm not here to impress you but to impress upon you that when the lens is wide open, example f/2 this is the "speed" of the lens. Anything wider than f/2.8 is considered a fast lens. You see, you might bump into someone and they ask how fast is your lens? Now you know the answer to that! It's wide open on your lens. Example f/2.8 or f/1.4.

Okay, time to do the photo essay on the "Aperture". Once you finish the set of exercises in the next chapter, you will have a greater understanding of the aperture than most; I guarantee you.

On the next page are a couple of examples to and educate. The photographer used a shallow depth of field probably around f/2 .8, to capture the baseball players.

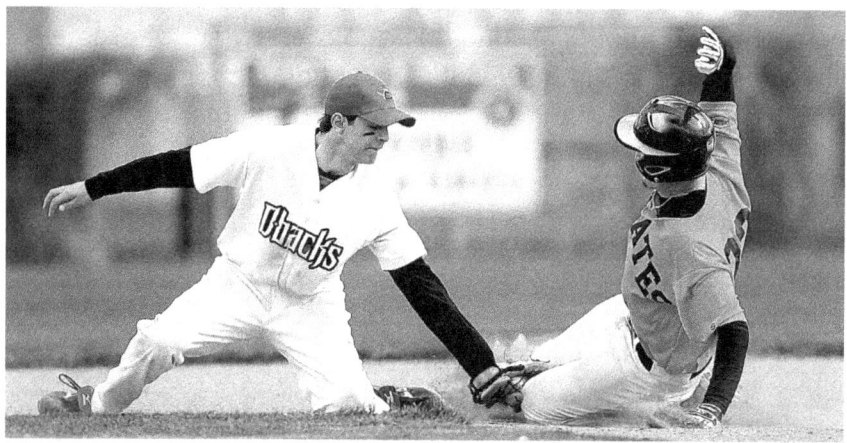

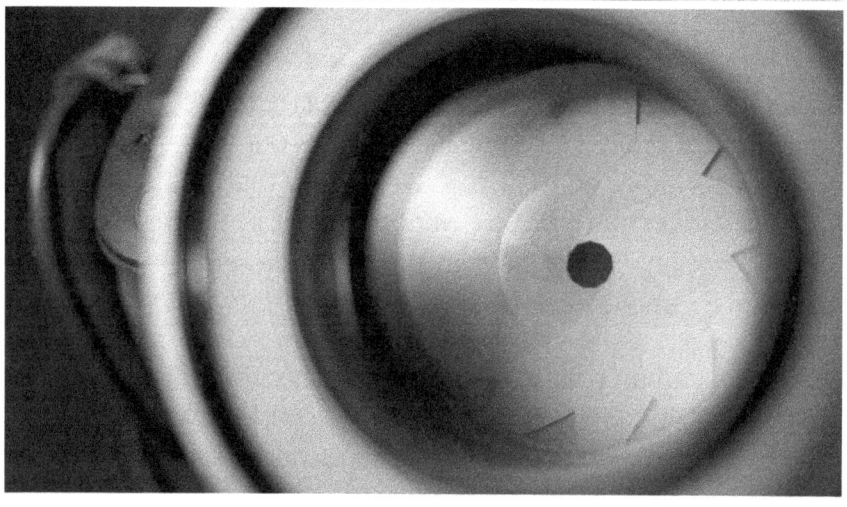

CHAPTER 13

Aperture Priority: A set of guided exercises

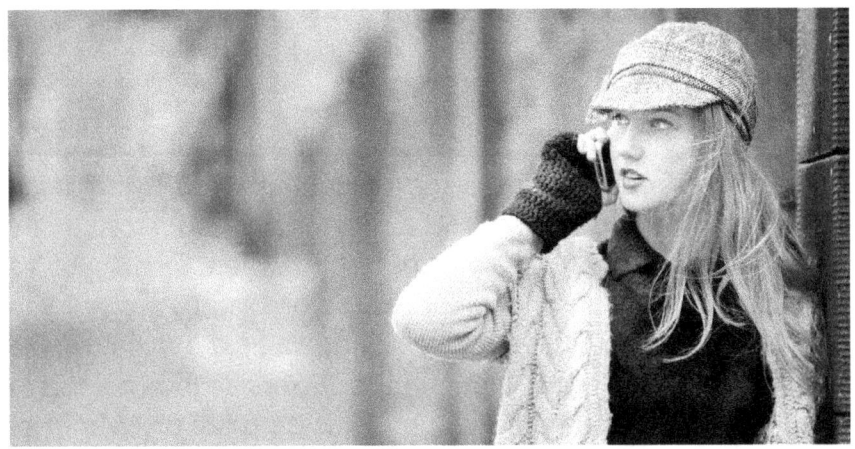

Shoot a roll and learn this creative camera control

Now that we have given you a greater understanding of how the aperture works, with this photo essay, you'll learn what it's most useful for and how to decide what aperture to use. The subject matter and story you want to convey to the viewer, will determine what aperture you choose.

So, for this shoot, you will need a model again. A friend, family member or partner will do, but this time, you don't need a bicycle or any props to achieve the result in this set of exercises. Please note, if you have a tripod it could be handy for this set of practices. If you don't own one, either borrow one or invest in one. You will often need it and for this exercise, your shutter speeds might be down to 1/4 of a second which means hand holding the camera will give you camera shake through the image. But if you have to hand hold the camera, that's okay. You will also have to put the camera continually down while you write in your log book in between scenes which is annoying as well. The ISO setting for today's set of exercises should be around about 800. You're going to put the camera mode dial to A, for Aperture priority. Now by doing so, you will decide what aperture to use, and your camera will compensate by choosing the shutter speed to give proper exposure. So in lots of ways you and the camera are working as a team but at least, I have you making decisions about which aperture to choose.

An environmental shoot

Now for this group of exercises I would like you to be in an environment where it is a street scene, maybe go into the city somewhere or down a leafy street. Somewhere where you've got a fence line or a shopping strip something that gives you repetition and depth. Here below is an example of what I'd like you to copy. The great thing about this exercise today is this is going to be very fast and profound. This group of tasks is what I call a static exercise. What I mean by static is that the subject doesn't move, all you are doing is composing the image, setting the aperture, making note what the shutter speed is doing, taking the capture and logging the results.

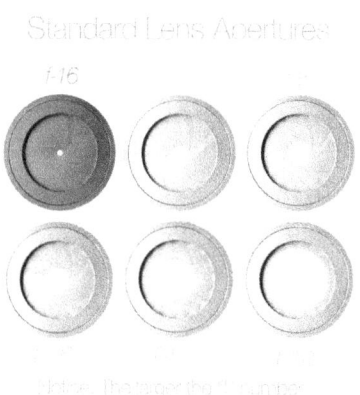

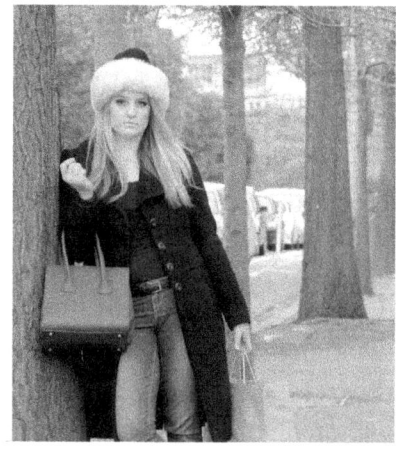

Please note: in the example images above and below you will notice how the background is influenced by using different aperture settings. Choosing f/16 (the image above) allows the background to be very distracting and it is reasonably hard to pick the subject from the background. Conversely, choosing f/2.8 (the image below) allows the viewer to immediately pick out the subject matter.

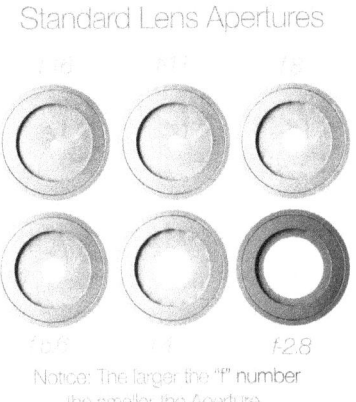

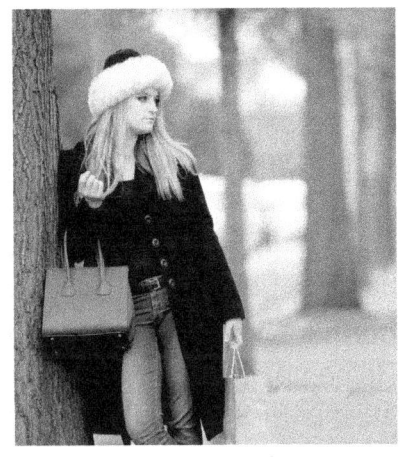

Put the aperture on f/16 and I would like your model to lean up against the fence line or post. And I'd like the image to be a three-quarter portrait. So what I mean by that is their head is nearly at the top of the frame, and you're going to cut them off just above their ankles. Now take two shots, one where they are looking directly at the camera (known as "on camera") and the second shot, profile looking into the negative space. What is negative space you ask? Sorry, again I tend to levitate over to the art side. If you look at the example above you'll notice that the subject is off to the left and not centred this is the most basic compositional consideration called the rule of thirds, or the Golden Mean. The negative space is the greatest amount of space where the subject should be looking. More of this will be in my book on compositional considerations. Now back to the task at hand.

Take note of what the shutter is doing

Once you've completed the two captures at f/16, take careful note of what the camera has chosen for the shutter speed. It might be around an 8th, a15th or a 30th. Now log the information into your book and "open up the aperture" to f/11 and I want you to notice what the shutter speed is doing now. If your D-SLR or Mirrorless camera is like most on the planet, your shutter speed will now be faster. So if it were on a 15th, it should be around about a 30th now. Also, a moment ago I asked you to "Open up the Aperture." I'm using photographic jargon, why? Because I want you to get used to the idea of speaking in this language. More and more as you start to understand these terms or jargon and they become part of your vocabulary you'll notice that you become better at photography. Moving on I would like you just to keep photographing the subject in a three-quarter portrait until you have opened up the aperture to "wide open". Remember, "wide open" is as far as the lens aperture can open example f/2 or f/2.8. If you're using a zoom lens, it might be f/3.5 or f/4.

Now for the fun bit, the download

Go through the same procedure as you did for the shutter exercises and what you're going to notice will be profound. Import the images into the photo editor that shows metadata. Open up your logbook and just check that what you had written down when you took the photograph is marrying up with the metadata. Once you have established that your logbook is accurate, I would like you to open up the images in the photo management app, so that you can zoom fullscreen on each picture. Start from capture one where you had the aperture on f/16. But I don't want you to take much notice of the exposure because the camera helped expose the image pretty well. What I would like you to notice is how sharp the background is and particular things that are static in the background and how sharp they are. Now I would like you to do the same for f/11, f/8, etc. all the way to "wide open".

Okay, what you'll notice as you open up the aperture more and more is how sharp the subject looks and how the background becomes more blurry or out of focus. In photography, this is commonly known as depth of field. The "depth of field" is effectively the zone of sharpness that you should expect at a given aperture. An easy way of remembering how much "zone of sharpness" you have is the greater the f-number, an example is f/11, the wider zone of sharpness, or deeper depth of field. Conversely, the smaller the number example f/4 the smaller zone of sharpness, or shallow depth of field. Now, this stuff is excellent to know because now you have a vital tool or camera control at your disposal that can separate your subject from the background at a moments notice. Just by making a decision to open up the aperture. Your iPhone can't do that, nor can the typical point-and-shoot camera. Can you see how understanding the aperture becomes very useful and empowering! Most amateurs never take the time or go to the effort to learn this incredible camera control. Now for the first time, you have the ability to capture what is in front of you exactly the way you see it with your own eyes.

Make sure you write in your journal

Now at this point, it would be a very good idea if you take a moment and write in your journal. I think you should go over all the images again from this exercise, starting at f/16 right through to wide open and write down what you see and what you've learned, etc. Tomorrow morning upon awakening, read your journal again on what you had written. Whether it was a sentence, a paragraph or 10 pages. At this point, you must have a greater understanding, and I believe like never before with your camera controls. This my friend is commonly known as one of those "wow" moments.

You should be proud of yourself because you have been disciplined and diligent in reading this book firstly, but then adhering to the photo essay exercises and logging all the data accurately after each shoot.

Now let's look at one other clever control that will make your image making easier. It's called the exposure compensation dial.

I'll look forward to seeing you in the next chapter.

CHAPTER 14

Exposure compensation function

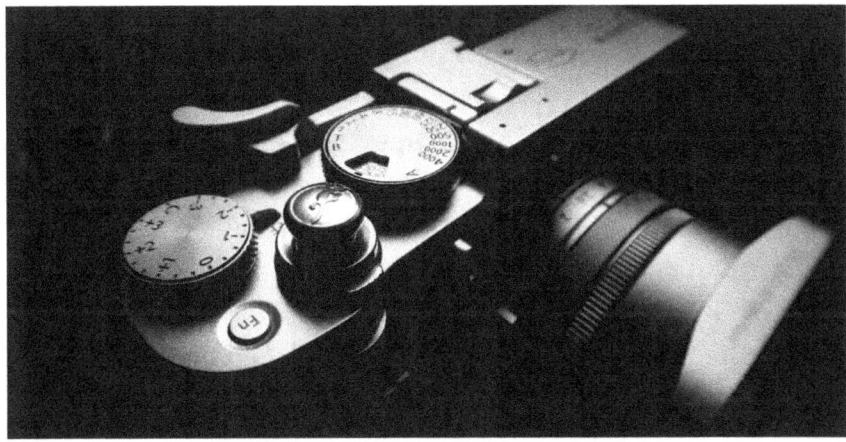

A very handy dial

Another creative camera control that we should be looking at before we get into manual mode is the exposure compensation dial. I'm not a tremendous fan of this when I'm shooting with my Nikon, but I must admit, I do use this camera control when I'm shooting "Aperture Priority" with my mirrorless camera. Which is the Fuji X Pro1.

There are a lot of amateur photographers out there that use this function habitually. If you don't happen to be one of them or you only use it occasionally, it would be expedient to dive into it, so let's explore it.

The exposure compensation dial is there to quickly adjust exposure, "on the fly". The dial is situated on most cameras generally on the top right-hand side at the top, nearly always next to the shutter button. I know on the Canon & Nikon the exposure compensation button is on the right-hand side on the top. It is positioned there on my Fuji, also. The increments are generally one-third of a stop. These figures indicate fractional stops, and you can usually increase or decrease exposure with this dial from 1 to 4 stops. When you're looking through the lens and if you are under pressure to take a major photograph, you can instantly adjust the exposure with this dial. A very handy creative camera control, when time is of the essence. Let me give you an example of when you would use the exposure compensation dial.

When shooting in all auto modes, Aperture Priority, Shutter Priority and Program Mode. Please note: when you move into a full Manual Mode the exposure compensation dial has no effect. So this is why I am choosing to cover it now before we get into manual mode. The fact is, the internal light meter that is recording correct exposure does a fabulous job and is accurate most of the time. However, it is taking in the whole scene and doing an average exposure reading. So if most of the scene you are photographing is light, the meter will go "wow", there is a lot of light so I will stop down to compensate. Smart hey? No! Because the image now will be dark, or underexposed. Vice versa if the scene happens to have a lot of dark tones (low key). Ah, this is when the exposure compensation dial mode comes into its own.

With some of the small mirrorless cameras, for example, the Fuji X-Pro1 or the Leica MP 240 rangefinder, the exposure compensation dial is very handy. Because you can look through the viewfinder, take a shot, view the capture on the electronic viewfinder, without ever removing your eye, and see whether the exposure is under or over. Now let's say that you have underexposed the image by a 1/3 of a stop, you can quickly adjust the exposure compensation dial by increasing the exposure by 1/3 of a stop. Do another test capture until the exposure is accurate and then blaze away. Now this again is without ever taking your eye away from the viewfinder. This technique is incredibly fast and also very accurate.

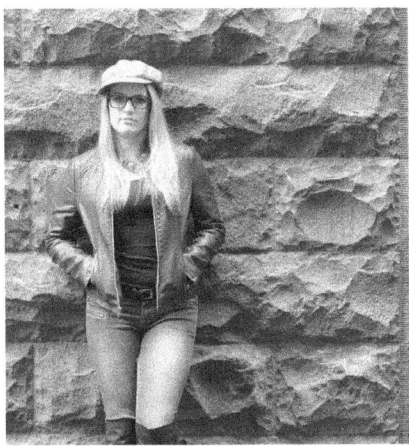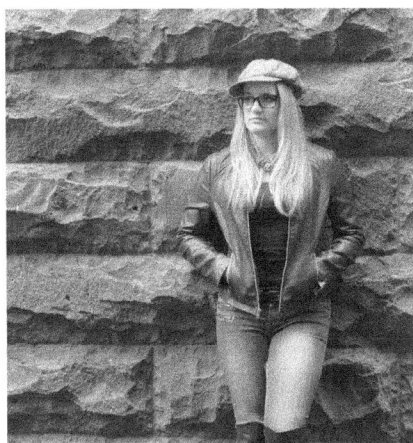

Above is a perfect example of how the subject (left) is against a dark blue stone wall and the internal light metre is just taking an average reading. Because the scene is dark it lightens up the bluestone wall and hence, the subject is a bit overexposed. On the image on the (right above) I use the exposure compensation dial and dialled it one third (1/3) of a stop less exposure. It looks better exposed overall than the one on the left.

As I mentioned earlier, I have the Fuji X pro1, which is mirrorless, and this is the same technique that I use when I need to get the right exposure fast. I never take my eye away from the viewfinder. So you wouldn't see me in the field, like most amateur photographers who take a shot then look at the back of the LCD screen straight after, then take another shot, look at the LCD, etc., several times. The fact is ladies and gentlemen, by the time you check the LCD screen four or five times, the chances are the subject you are photographing is long gone. Mind you; I see rank amateurs, right through to seasoned pro's doing this all the time.

When you're shooting moving pictures or candid photography,

and you notice that the image is slightly under or over you can quickly adjust for exposure by just dialling up or down with the exposure compensation dial, which happens to be right next to the shutter button. That way you are not fumbling for the shutter. A very quick way of checking your exposure when shooting with your Mirrorless camera or a D-SLR would be, using the internal exposure meter to take a test capture. Check the back of the LCD and then if you are in the ballpark, you can adjust up or down a third of the stop with the exposure compensation dial, and boom, you're ready to blaze away.

This function could be your best friend

Remember, all the tools on your camera, knobs and buttons are there for a reason. What I've also found over the years is that most photographers when out on a shoot operate differently. I believe this single camera control dial could end up being your best friend, particularly if you're out on location or covering some event like perhaps a child's birthday party, a sporting event or even some sort of newsworthy events where you're under pressure. Remember; I want you to have full control over the image-making and hence that is why you're going to be shooting in full manual mode. Just like ISO, the shutter, and the aperture, the exposure compensation dial must be exercised to understand it correctly.

Below is a short training session to understand the exposure compensation dial.

Please note: Like every other exercise, after every shot is taken I would like you to write down the settings. That way when you download the images, it becomes crystal clear what the exposure compensation dial is doing. You also want to be able to refer to your notes at any point.

Please do not skip this exercise on this creative function as this is an important part of the process of mastering your camera controls.

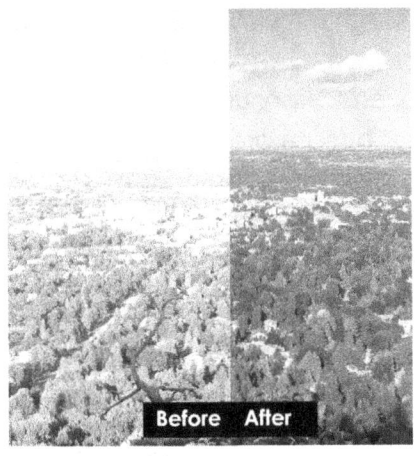
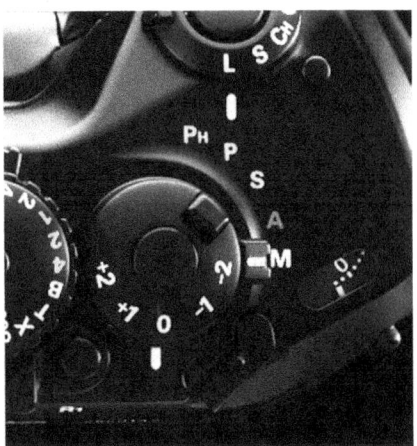

Exposure Compensation Exercise

Now for the sake of this exercise, you can pretty much choose any subject you like. And I think we will do three various topics, just to make sure you've got a greater understanding of how this dial works.

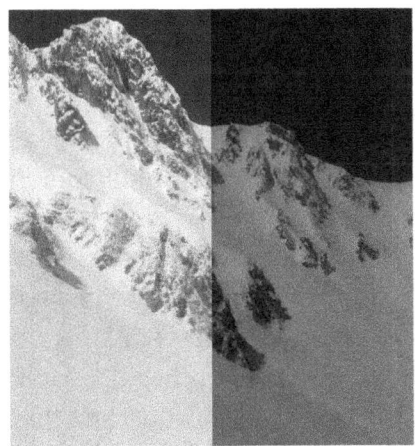
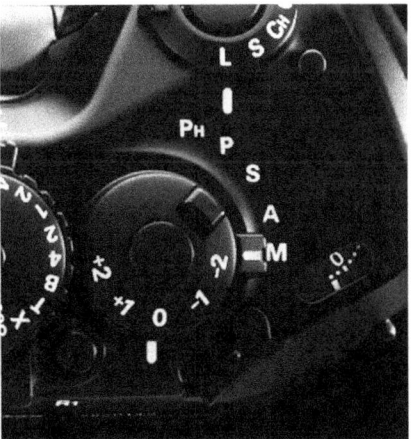

At this point, this will be the last exercise using auto settings.

Please keep your function dial to "Aperture Priority" mode (same as last chapter). Adjust your ISO to 800, aperture to f/5.6 and your shutter speed to 1/250th. Now point the camera at your first subject. I now want you to look through the viewfinder and at the (HUD) head up display, where you see all of the functions and settings of shutter speed, aperture, and exposure meter. Now the goal of this exercise is to get the exposure pretty much correct for the first capture. What this means is that the pointer should be right in the middle, around zero. So looking through the lens adjust the aperture or shutter or both to get the exposure meter needle around zero.

Okay, let's take the capture by pressing the shutter button. And let's have a look at the result. Now if you have done this correctly, your exposure should be reasonably accurate. So have a look at the LCD on the back of the camera and see how close the exposure is. Now for the interesting part. While you're looking through the viewfinder, put your forefinger on the exposure compensation dial. Now if the exposure was slightly over exposed turn the dial .3 into the minus direction and what you should notice in the viewfinder is how that compensates on the exposure meter to where exposure is about spot on. Now take another capture. Have another look at the LCD on the back of the camera and what you should notice is the exposure looks very good.

Just so you get an understanding for the exposure compensation dial fully, I would like you to look now through the viewfinder again and turn the dial another minus .3. You'll notice that the exposure meter is illustrating that the image is now slightly underexposed. Now take another shot, have a look at the LCD screen. Now do it again, another -.3 and keep doing this until you are -2 stops, and you'll notice that the image on the LCD is dark. You'll find that most exposure compensation dials go -2 stops and +2 stops for rangefinder cameras and 3 to 4 stops for D-SLR's. Okay, go back to your original exposure where it was in the middle by moving the exposure compensation dial back to 0. take a shot and log the information. Now you are going to start to move the dial +.3 and take a shot. Notice that the image on the back of the LCD screen is lighter, or slightly overexposed. At this point, write the information down. Continually move the dial +.3 after each shot and log the information until you are +2 stops.

I also would like you to make note of what is happening with the shutter speeds at this point. Once you have concluded this set of exercises, you are ready to move on to the real deal, the big game.

You are well on your way

In closing, I would just like to say that if you have followed me up to now, have read every word, applied the learnings and logged the information I am very proud of you. You are now well on your way to being in the top 10% of amateur photographers around the world and for that, you should be proud. Let's move into the big arena now where you have full control over the picture taking!

Yes, that's right, it's time to adjust the function dial to M, for manual mode. From this moment on your photography is going to go quantum. Don't be surprised if you find photographing in manual mode easy. The chances are if you are like most amateurs you have the ability to understand and photograph in full manual mode. This now means that you'll photograph and capture what you see, and how you see it, exactly.

Get excited! Looking forward to seeing you in the next chapter!

CHAPTER 15

Putting it all together

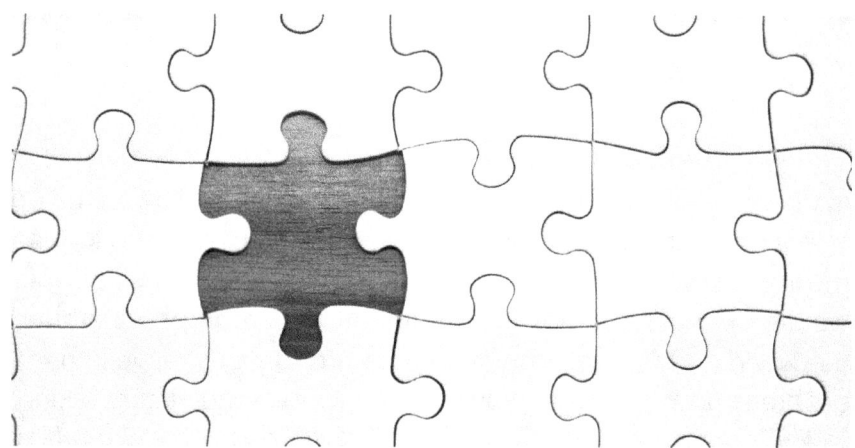

The prelude to controlling your
camera in full manual mode

If you've been disciplined, have read each chapter and applied the learnings by doing the exercises you are ready for the crescendo. This, my friends, is "putting it all together", controlling your camera in manual mode. Okay, without further ado, I present to you the chapter that's going to change your photographic life forever. So on the mode dial, you're looking for the M, which in previous chapters you know already. Move the dial to M and from this moment on you'll never look back.

Now at this point, one of two things is going to happen.

1. You're feeling excited, empowered and ready to go to full manual controls on your D-SLR or your mirrorless camera.
2. You're nervous as hell, and you're asking yourself, "Have I skipped anything leading up to now? Did I complete all

the exercises? Do I have a full understanding of how the "aperture priority" and also shutter priority work?"

What I know is with this planet spinning faster on a daily basis, a lot of people are time poor, and it's very easy to skip or skim over things. This, however, can sometimes be false economy if it means you have to go back and revise some of the techniques that you did in the past. I'm sure you're not one of them.

Enjoy this journey that you are about to embark on

Remember, the journey is just as exciting as the destination and we are nearly always at our happiest when we are learning. Mind you, it is not much fun if you have to backtrack and try and work out what part you skipped. Without sounding militant, what I suggest is go back through the shutter speed and aperture sections, check your notes and make sure that you haven't skipped anything. This will speed up the understanding when going to full manual mode, and also, it will empower you knowing full well that you have spent the time learning the controls on this magnificent computer, digital capture device, commonly referred to as a camera.

Before I set out the photographic exercises for full manual mode, I would like to ask a favour. If you've never photographed in manual mode before and this is your first time, I believe that it would be worth employing, either a family member or friend and a few props like hats scarves bicycles, flowers, a pet dog, etc. This work will be very artistic if you include some or all of the suggestions above.

Putting it altogether. You're ready for full manual mode

In the next chapter, I'm going to list a series of photographs I would like you to take. Each picture is designed to maximise your learning in the shortest space of time. Even though you are going to be in manual mode, a lot of the focus will be around the aperture. Now, I'll be asking you to take specific images with a specific aperture, example f/8, then you'll be asked to take the same photograph but wide open, example f/2.8. Every time you're changing the aperture, you obviously have to compensate with the shutter speed to achieve the correct exposure. Up till now, your versatile camera has adjusted this for you. Now it's up to you to adjust all camera controls. So if you are opening up the aperture by two full stops you're going to have to speed up the shutter by two full stops. So, let's look at an example, shall we? When you're out in the environment and let's say you have your ISO set to 800. And when you're pointing the camera down the street the correct exposure is 250th at f/8. Now I'm going to ask you to open up the aperture by two stops. Which would be what? That's right f/4.

Now if you left everything the same and you took a test capture and looked at the back of the LCD screen, you would notice everything would be washed out because you have overexposed the scene by two stops. To achieve correct exposure, we must compensate by speeding up the shutter speed by two stops. So the 250th becomes 1000th. (Just a mental note here, one stop is doubling or halving the aperture or shutter speed). If you were to take a test capture now, you would notice the exposure will be close to spot on. So once you complete this set of 10 specific images, you can have the opportunity then to take a series of your photographs while you're out there.

Perhaps first write down at least half a dozen different scenes that you want to shoot. Below are a few examples of suggestions.

- Walk scene with the dog (walking towards camera)
- Walk scene with an umbrella (open and closed, walking towards camera)
- Leaning against a fence line or wall (subject looking at the camera - "on camera")
- Leaning against a fence line or wall ("off camera" - subject is looking approximately 30 degrees away from the camera)

- Back shot walking away from the camera
- Cafe scene drinking coffee, reading the paper, looking around

Now these are just a few suggestions and of course, I am visualising all of these scenes in black and white as they would look very artful in that genre. Especially if you are using a longer lens (say 200mm) and keeping your aperture nearly wide open to give you a really shallow depth of field.

In Chapter One "So what's the difference between a good photographer and a great photographer" I talk about how it's paramount to be fully integrated and understand both your camera controls and also being able to see photographically and understand composition. Without getting ahead of myself too much, I do want to touch on seeing photographically and also composition. The reason is that I want you to already have a goal in mind before you start to shoot in full manual mode. The few specific images I would like you to take along with a few scenes I have suggested above are there for a specific reason.

Pre-Visualisation

Let's take the first one which is a walking scene with the dog (walking towards camera). I would like you to close your eyes for a moment then visualise this scene. In photographic terms, this is commonly known as pre-visualisation. It means you can already see the final capture before you've even got out there and shot it. Very powerful tool when you harness it. In this scene where is the subject looking? At the camera or scanning their head around? What are they wearing? Do they have a swagger or do they have a saunter? Apart from walking, what else is the dog doing? Smiling, tongue out or panting? Is the dog in control or is it pulling on its lead and jumping around like an untrained seal! Hmm, there are lots of things to consider and think about when you are designing and also directing a scene.

So what's the difference between pre-visualising a scene and executing it in auto settings compared to capturing it in full Manual Mode? In a nutshell, whatever you have pre-visualised you'll be able to put that exact scene on film with Manual Mode. Whereby having the camera on Auto you might miss it by a bunch, because you and the camera are not one. Now I hope it doesn't sound too deep, but I must point out that from this moment on, you will take your photography to a whole new level, and also you will take it more seriously. I also would like to point out your work will give you the greatest pleasure because it will be much more aesthetically pleasing to the eye. Especially when you start getting "Wows" from your family and friends as they see your work improving out of sight.

By having full control for the first time, over the camera, you are now like the master painter, who can brush in those subtle colours and directional light.

Now, as in previous chapters, I'm going to ask you to write in your logbook every capture you take. This new set of exercises will be a mix of guided exercises by me and also a free-form set of exercises as well. The important thing here is to read the chapter on the practices before you choose your models and props. This way you'll be better prepared for the exercises, and you also enjoy the shoot much more.

Recruiting family members or friends

Now if it's possible, I would also suggest bringing an assistant along. Yeah, this could be a younger brother or sister or another friend, etc. The idea of having the assistant is to get you to concentrate more on what you need to achieve during the shoot and so your mind is very clear and uncluttered. Not to mention, if this is the first time you have put your camera on the full manual mode you also might be slightly nervous any assistance can help alleviate a lot of the stress. The most important task the assistant will have is asking you after every capture, what were the settings so they can log the information for you. Remember this is a hobby and you're supposed to be having fun. Your assistant will help you achieve that, if they log the info, etc.

Okay, I think we're ready to move on to the next chapter. This set of exercises will be incredibly empowering, and your photography will never be the same. As I was growing up and there were times during my school years when I was having trouble with my homework. Example, algebra. I would be stressed and frustrated because I couldn't work out the answers. My father would often say to me, "Darren, everything is easy... when you know how." What a simple but profound statement.

The reason I share that with you is once you've gone through this next shoot, done all the exercises, downloaded the work and looked back don't be surprised if you say to yourself "that was easy". Why? Once you are photographing in the full manual mode you'll never go back to auto settings; I guarantee you.

Below are a couple of my images to inspire you!

I would like you to take special note about what aperture and shutter speeds I might have used to create this artwork.

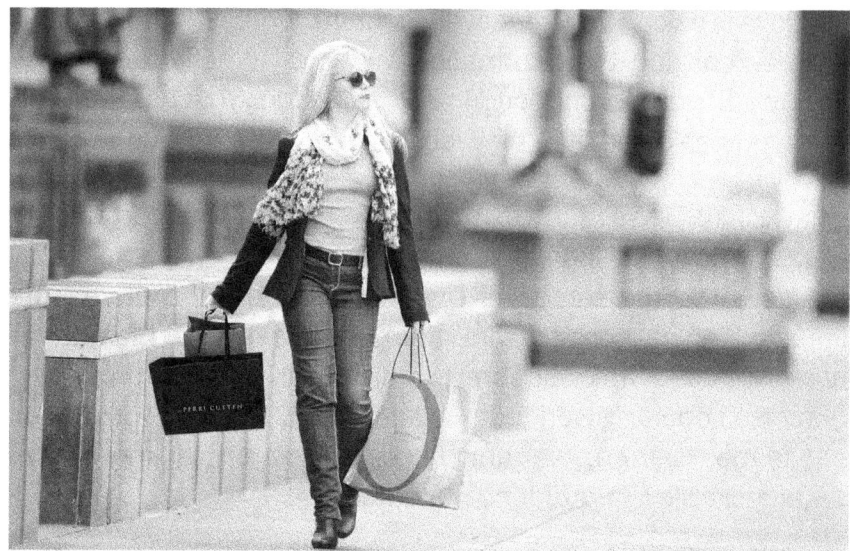

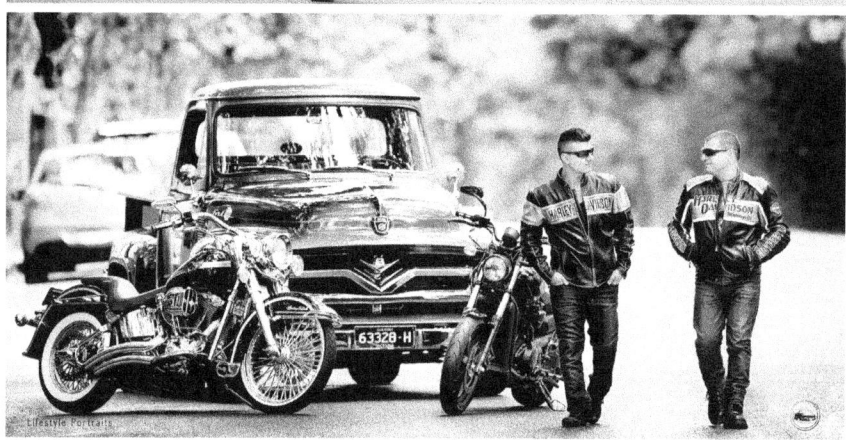

Let's go to the next chapter and as our good friends at Nike say, "Just do it!"

CHAPTER 16

Mastering the camera controls in manual mode

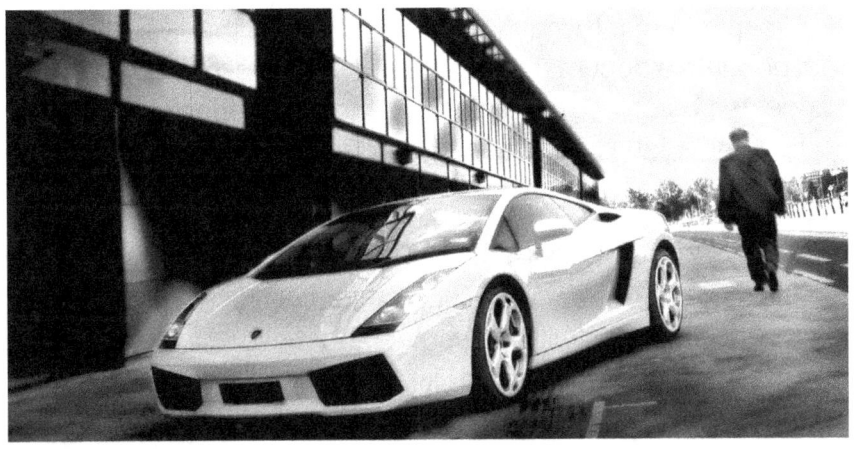

Now, you're on your way to being in the top 10%

Before we begin the set of exercises, firstly I want to congratulate you! All the previous tasks and also logging the captures and information has all led to this. Your moment of glory awaits you! Why? because this is where your image making will go through the roof. You are in full control of the scene now. Remember, nothing changes; I still would like you to log in your book every shot you take for this photo essay.

One quick word about the set of exercises below. I have consciously made each scene with a different aperture, and you'll be changing the aperture continuously during this photo essay. In unison, you will also be changing the shutter speed to compensate for correct exposure. So it might make you feel like you're going back and forth, back and forth but that's the whole idea to gain some momentum using a repetitive process. Also, you'll have an excellent handle on exposing manually by the end of today's efforts.

Onto the task at hand. This particular set of exercises must be shot accurately.

To do it properly you could do one of a couple of things here with the set of tasks. One way would be to bring this book with you and keep referring to it during the session. Another way would be to type it into a document and print it out and take it with you. As I suggested before, you still must log the information so that when you download the shoot, each capture will have a distinct look.

Shooting out on location

On the set, while shooting, I suggest that you use a monopod or even a tripod as this will free you up and make you more mobile. The set of images that I would like you to photograph are all to be taken vertically, or (portrait orientation, not horizontal, as below). Now take a test capture after checking out the camera exposure meter. Set the ISO to 800. Make sure the camera you are using is configured to autofocus and is on "single" shot which means when you focus and hold down the shutter button halfway and change the composition by moving the camera slightly; it will stay focused on whatever subject you are photographing. Put the aperture on f/11 and now adjust the shutter speed until the exposure meter is suggesting it is the correct exposure. Take a test capture, Check the LCD screen and see if you're happy with the exposure and focus. If so, proceed.

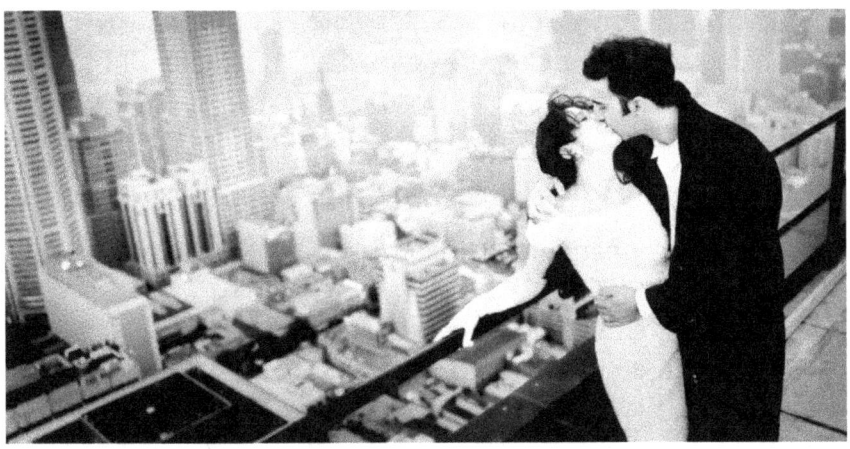

Scene 1 (On camera)

- Camera orientation vertical (portrait)
- Aperture (f/11)
- Shutter speed adjusted
- Three-quarter framing

Your model is leaning against the wall or fence line, and I would like you to crop this to a three-quarter shot. So you want just a little bit of headroom above their head, and you want to crop just below the calves. They are looking at the camera. Take the capture. Check the LCD screen for focus and exposure. If you are happy with the image, Log the information into your workbook.

Scene 2 (Off camera)

- Camera orientation vertical (portrait)
- Aperture wide open (f/2.8)
- Shutter speed adjusted
- Three-quarter framing

Your model is still leaning against the wall or fence line, and this is still a three-quarter crop. In fact, I would like you to take two captures of this scene. The first image is going to be an exact duplicate of scene one where they are looking directly at the camera. The second picture you take of this scene is where they are looking away from camera (known as "off camera") heading towards a profile shot.

Scene 3 (On and off camera)

- Camera orientation vertical (portrait)
- Aperture (f/5.6)
- Shutter speed adjusted
- Full-length framing

This time, your model is still leaning against the wall or fence-line casually, and this is to be a full-length crop. Two images are to be taken again. The first picture is looking at the camera and the second image is looking off-camera.

Scene 4 (Off camera and full profile)

- Camera orientation vertical (portrait)
- Aperture wide open (f/2.8)
- Shutter speed adjusted
- Full-length framing

Again you're going to be taking two images. We're going to mix this up just a little bit, so it isn't the same as scene three. For the first image, we want them to have a conversation with you, so they are looking about 20° off-camera, away from the wall or fence they are leaning on. Then I would like you to take a full profile shot for the second image in the same direction as image one.

Make sure that you are logging the information into your workbook!

Scene 5 (On camera and off camera)

- Camera orientation vertical (portrait)
- Aperture (f/8)

- Shutter to be adjusted
- Pictorial framing

Now in this set of images, I'm going to suggest framing the image pictorially. Okay, so what do I mean by pictorially? A pictorial image is basically where the subject matter only represents a small percentage of the picture, let's say only 50% of the whole image. So if you're using a zoom lens, you're going to reduce the focal length. If it is a fixed lens like a telephoto lens then you will have to move back or, ask your subject to move back. So when you look through the viewfinder, your model should only represent around 50% of the frame.

This again is a static shot leaning against the wall or fence-line. I suggest that you take two images for scene five. The first photo can be looking down the barrel at the camera and then take the second picture. This time, take it off camera or even heading towards profile.

If you have been following the rules of engagement so far, you would have logged all five scenes. The recorded data will be invaluable when you download the information. All being well if there hasn't been too much light fluctuation the exposures should be quite constant and on the money. What will be interesting for you, is how the subject separates from the background as soon as you start to open up the aperture and use a shallow depth of field.

Time to take you to a new level. We're going to create five new scenes. All of the scenes are going to have motion, moving pictures. So this set of exercises will be similar to what you've done so far, except your subject or model is going to be walking towards the camera. Now, if you did manage to bring a pet with you like a dog, they'll become an excellent prop at this point. If not, it doesn't matter. The main things here are to increase your awareness of using fast shutter speeds to stop movement, and also gain a greater understanding of using the aperture.

Last reminder: Have you been back to your retailer?

Before moving into the next exercises, you must change your autofocus to "tracking". Also, make sure that the autofocus is on continuous so you can take several shots in one burst. So when I say tracking, it means that the camera will continuously focus on moving subjects. Your trip back to the dealership or camera store would've unveiled this missing detail during your session with them. At this point, you must have a very clear understanding of how to change your autofocus to tracking now. Take a couple of test capture bursts (6 to 8 image bursts should do it). Do a quality check on your tracking function of your autofocus system. Check and make sure that it is following the subject and keeping the subject in focus. If you have done a "quality check" on this and you are sure that all the images are in focus, then let's begin.

Scene 6 (On or off camera)

- Camera orientation vertical (portrait)
- Aperture (f/16)
- Shutter to be adjusted
- Pictorial framing

Before you take the first capture, I would like you to take a test capture to make sure that the exposure is perfect. Now I wouldn't be surprised if your shutter speed is down to around a 30th, a 15th, or even an 8th of a second. If that's the case, you might need to increase your ISO from 800 to 1,600 or even more. Why? Because if you are shooting at a 30th or even a 15th of a second, the subject will probably have motion blur. So we need shutter speeds of at least a 60th or faster, to stop the action. Also, in this set of images, you're going to be taking several captures at the same time, one after the other using your inbuilt motor drive. With my Nikon D4, I can take 10 or 15 frame bursts per second when capturing motion. So direct your model to start slowly walking towards the camera and fire away. Make anywhere between 6 to 10 image captures.

Scene 7 (Off camera)

- Camera orientation vertical (portrait)
- Aperture wide open (f/2.8)
- Shutter speed to be adjusted
- Pictorial framing

We're going to take that walking scene again. However, you're going to have the lens wide-open this time. The autofocus is on continuous, so as your model is walking towards the camera, the autofocus should be picking them up sharply. Just to mix things up a bit, direct your subject to be looking away from the camera 30 to 60° left or right, so you have a different look to the last scene we did. In the download, and when you look at your logged information, you'll find this particular set of captures very rewarding. The images will have a special quality that is attractive and also very professional looking.

Scene 8 (On or off camera)

- Camera orientation vertical (portrait)
- Aperture wide open (f/2.8)
- Shutter speed to be adjusted
- Full-length start finishing to a 3/4 length framing

In this scene, we're not going to change the aperture. Let's leave it wide open and start your model around the full-length mark in the frame. Direct them to slowly start walking and start taking captures. Finish off when they are around the 3/4 length or three-quarter mark in the frame. Your stylised option here is whether you want them looking straight down the barrel of the camera, or you want them looking off camera across the street. Log the information. In the download, this again will be another fascinating set of captures. Especially from the very first frame, where the subject is full-length, and then where the subject is three-quarter length in the last frame. As the subject walks closer to the camera, you'll notice that the background will become more out of focus. The reason for this is, as the subject becomes closer to the camera, the depth of the field becomes more shallow. Hence, the background becomes blurry.

Scene 9 (On or off camera)

- Camera orientation vertical (portrait)
- Aperture (f/8)
- Shutter speed to be adjusted
- Full-length start finishing to a 3/4 framing

This sequence of captures is the same as scene eight, except this time we've set the aperture to f/8. Now you will notice that perhaps, this image will not be as strong compositionally. Part of the reason for that is that the background will become more distracting. So when you compare this picture to scene eight, you will notice a remarkable difference. This is especially noticeable at the start of these first few frames. The reason is that the depth of field is now deep, where nearly everything stays in focus. So the background is going to be competing with the subject at the start. However, as they come closer to the camera, and it becomes a three-quarter frame you'll find that the background will go out of focus and not compete. Again just like in scene eight you do have the option to either have your model looking straight down the barrel or they could be looking off camera.

This concludes this series of images and exercises

This doesn't mean that you have to stop photographing. Particularly, the fact that you have gone to a lot of effort and brought a friend or family member with you this would be a splendid time to create some imagery for them as well as for yourself. So feel free to practice and keep blazing away.

However, if you think you are done for the day, then let's keep moving.

Download imagery and archive

From this moment on, I want you to get the imagery back home and download it. Before you leave the location though, check that you have logged everything in your logbook. Again I would like you to compare what you have logged and what you see on your computer screen with the set of exercises outlined in this chapter. What you'll find will be critical in your decision-making in future picture taking. One perfect example is that in my industry, in Australia, they call me "Mr Wide Open". Why? Because I use a very shallow depth of field, in fact, most of the time I shoot with the lens aperture wide open. Most of my lenses are fast, around f/2.8. For years, I had a Leica 50mm f/1 lens and only ever shot with this lens wide open. This is one of the ways of keeping strong composition in all my portrait work. The subject stands out from the background. In my second book, in the series, I cover composition explicitly. One of the things I talk about in composition is your eye will always go to the sharpest part of an image. So by choosing a shallow depth of field, where the background is just blurred out, your eye is going to go to the subject every time, because it's the sharpest part of that photograph.

As in previous chapters, I would like you after you have downloaded and checked the logged information, to write in your journal about your findings. This journal will become history and in fact, you might hand it down to your children or you might just like to look at it and flashback every so often.

Technically, you have completed your learning on mastering the camera controls. However, personally, I think this is just the beginning for you, and I believe that your passion for photography will accelerate from this time on. You have conquered and completed the hardest part of photography which is the science side. And there are other aspects and factors to do with mirrorless and D-SLR cameras. And if you want to learn them, then do so for the fun of it. The fact is, as far as image making goes, you have worked through this book and series of lessons and exercises. As far as I am concerned you now have mastered the craft side of photography.

Well done, I salute you

Please turn over to the last chapter for a few closing words from me. Also, I would like to point you to a few resource sites that will get your juices flowing and inspire you to create art images that speak volumes.

CHAPTER 17

Prologue: The author's salutation to you

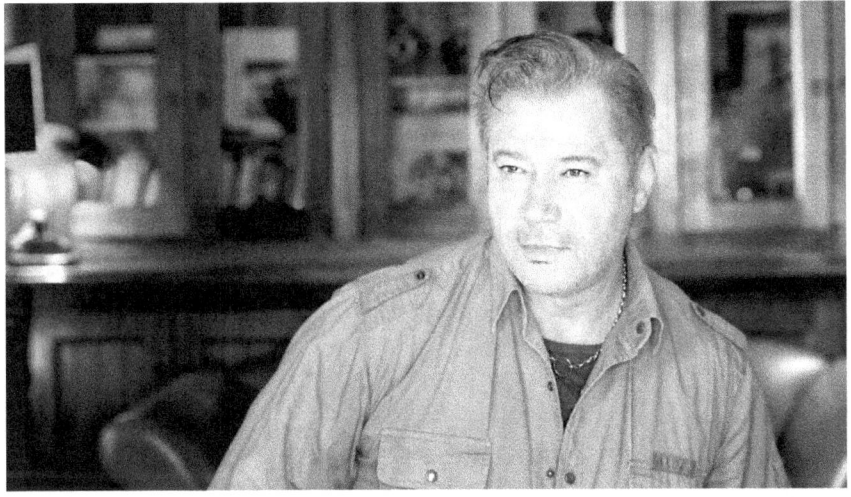

Well, this concludes the first book from me, for the amateur photographer.

So here we are my friend, we have reached your destination. Mastering the camera controls. However, in the scheme of things and the real world of photography, it has been a very short journey and may I add, a great one. Most amateurs never get this far in their photography. There are lots of reasons for that and probably also a few excuses, but you are in a different place. You're at the pinnacle.

In closing, I would just like to say that if you have been disciplined, logged all the information, completed all sets of exercises, you are well on your way to being in the top 10% of amateur photographers around the world. Understanding the mechanics and craft side of photography is an empowering place to be. By now you should be in control of your camera whether it happens to be a mirrorless or a D-SLR. What this means is every time you go out to either record an event or to capture images that interest you for your pleasure, you're going to get the technical aspect correct. Make sure you exercise the disciplines every time you're out photographing. It won't take long before this becomes second nature for you and you'll only ever choose the manual settings on your camera.

I would like to suggest that the guided group of exercises is now over. I would now like to indicate that you are in control of your creative image making from this moment on, and you can create either guided exercises or a photo essay to keep you on task and take your creativity to a whole new level. Here are a couple of ideas.

Create a photo essay of coffee culture in your town.

Create a photo essay of nature or landscapes with the theme being Serene.

Create a photo essay of a fashion item, example the hat or a bow tie or seamed stockings.

I think you get the idea. Get together with friends or family and do some mind-storming and come up with half a dozen challenges. If any of them enjoys photography and has a camera, go out together and then compare notes after you download. It's amazing how you start to see the world in a different way. All of a sudden, photographic opportunities present themselves, non-stop.

Lastly, I just wanted to share with you the way I work, every day, professionally. It outlines a set of procedures that I take before and during every shoot for my client. This also means that I do this for myself when I'm out and about shooting for pleasure.

The sequence of events

Below is a sequence of events that precedes nearly every shoot I do for every image I create. I suggest that you start with this procedure below and after awhile you'll probably come up with your own set of procedures. The very first question is the most important because this is going to help you to choose the appropriate camera controls to achieve the best result.

1. Ask yourself, what do I want to **capture** here?
2. Choose the **aperture**, whether you want shallow depth or not.
3. Check your meter on the top of the camera or LCD screen for **exposure.**
4. Adjust **shutter speed** and aperture accordingly.
5. Choose the correct auto **focus** setting: tracking or single shot.
6. **Compose** the image: check the background and framing.
7. Take a **test capture**, check for Focus and exposure
8. Put your finger on the trigger and **blaze away**.

If you need more help or inspiration, invest in my video series

"Mastering Your Camera Controls". I promise you, the video series will fast track you even more and leave no doubt in your mind about anything we have covered in this book. Also, when you register for the video series, you have the ability to send your top three images for me to personally critique. This is like having a photographic coach right there next to you and guiding you in the right direction. You can't put a price on this.

Lastly, a few resource sites to really get your juices flowing.

1. **Pinterest**: search Black and white photographic masters
2. **Youpic:** This site is for the amateur user that wants to share their work
3. **Instagram:** search topics that interest you most
4. **www.tilnak.com** or search Google images for Darren Tilnak

I suggest joining these resources and contributing to the vast bank of photography that is available around the world.

I have also included in the middle of this book and following a few images of mine. These particular images are some of my favourites from my archives of both my professional world and also my personal imagery. From what you've learnt in this book try and break down and work out how these images have been taken using the camera controls. This would be a very good start, so that every time you see an image that appeals to you online or in a gallery somewhere you can get some sort of indication of how the author produced that image. You should be able to gauge what shutter speed, aperture and focal length of the lens etc.

Until I see you in the video series, good shooting my fellow artist.

PS. Look out for my next book **"Master the 7 Keys to Composition".** All going well the book should be complete by late 2018.

Until we meet again, this is your photographic friend and coach signing off.

Darren Tilnak
www.tilnak.com
www.masteringphotography.com.au

CHAPTER 18
Portfolio: Professional artwork

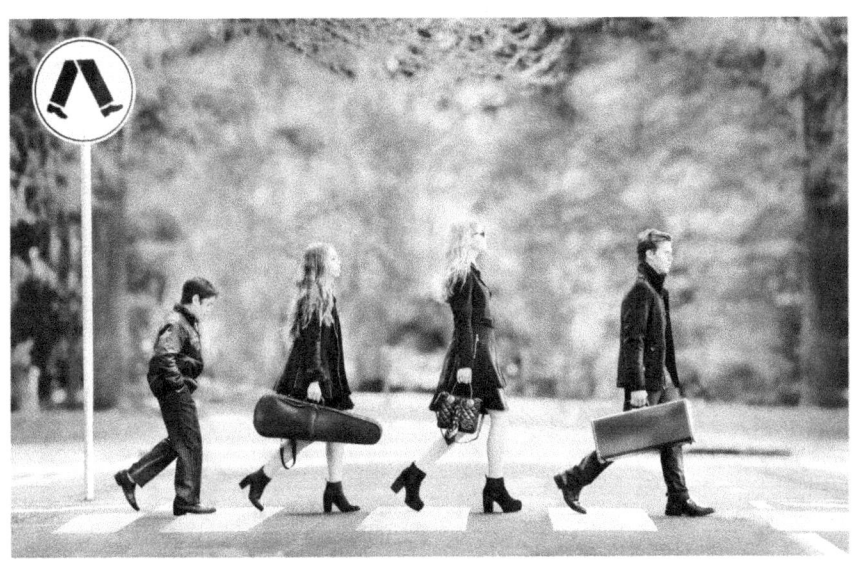

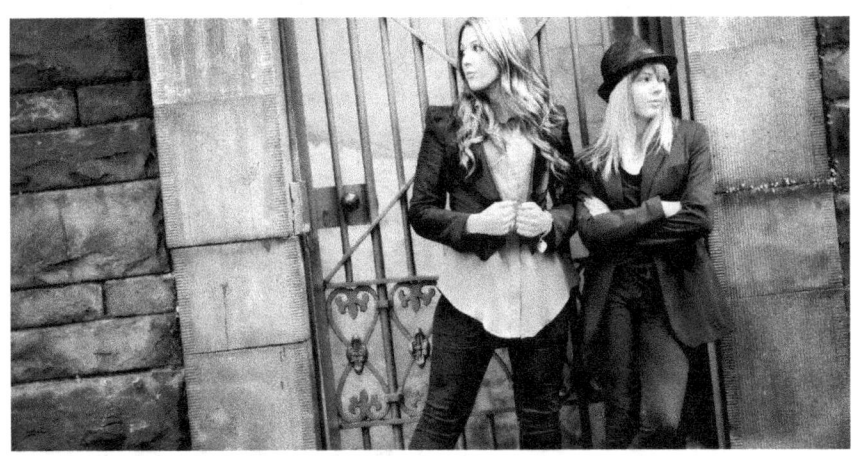

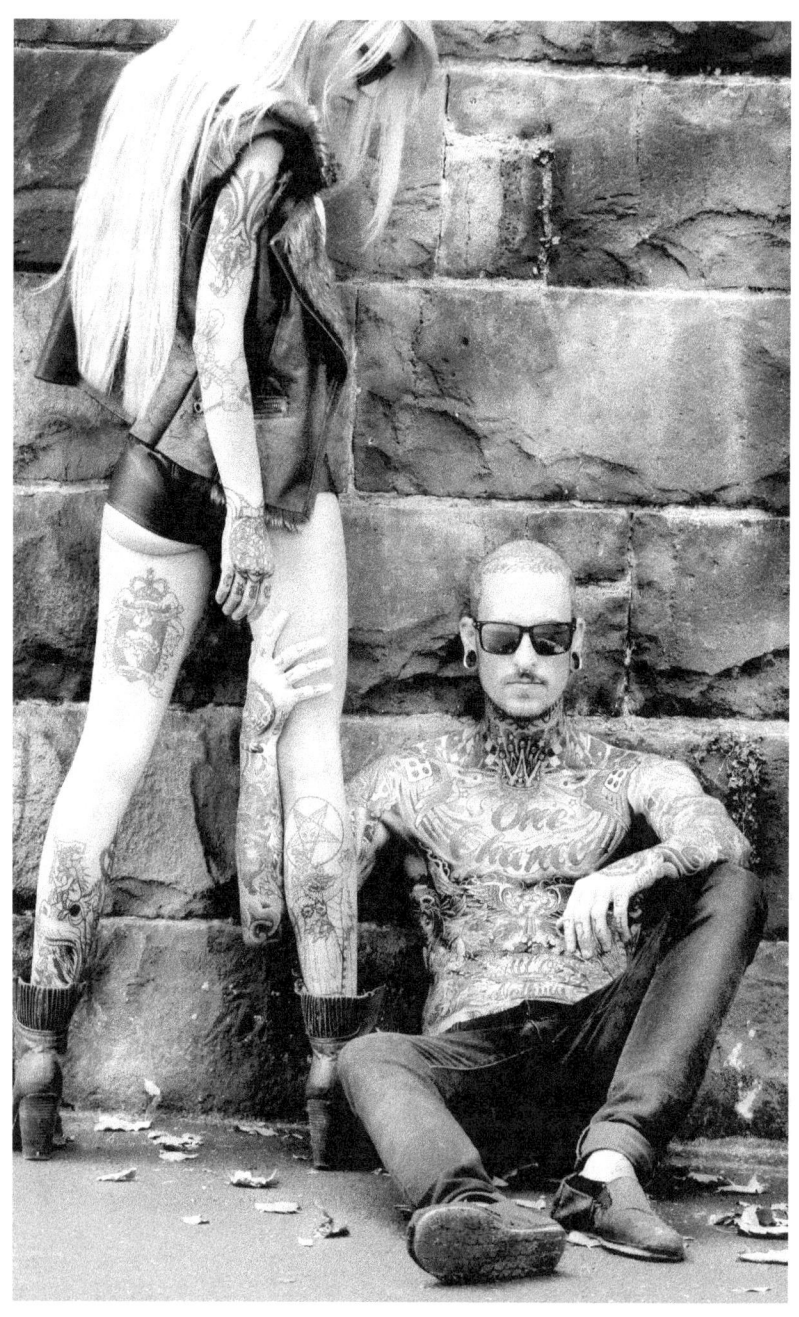

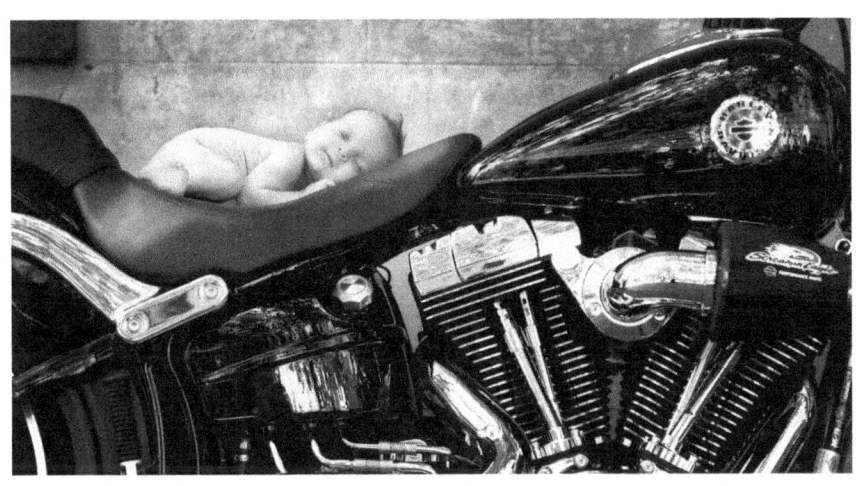

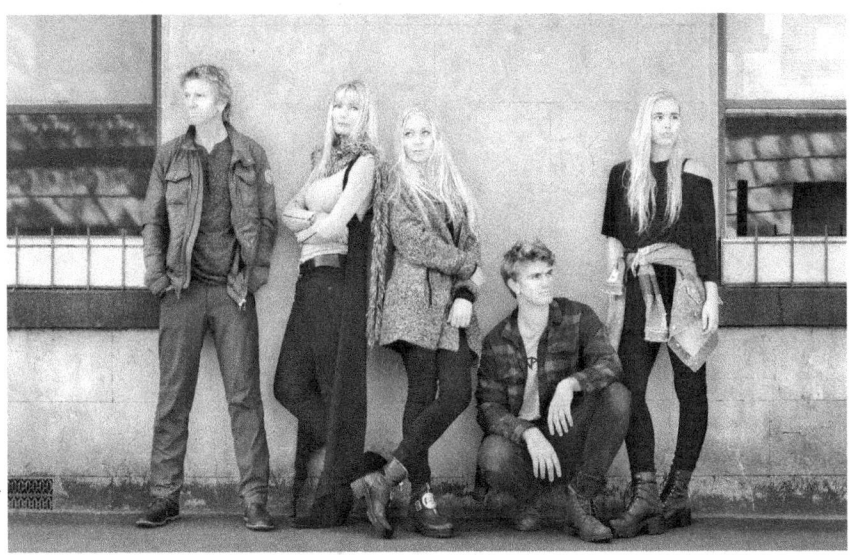

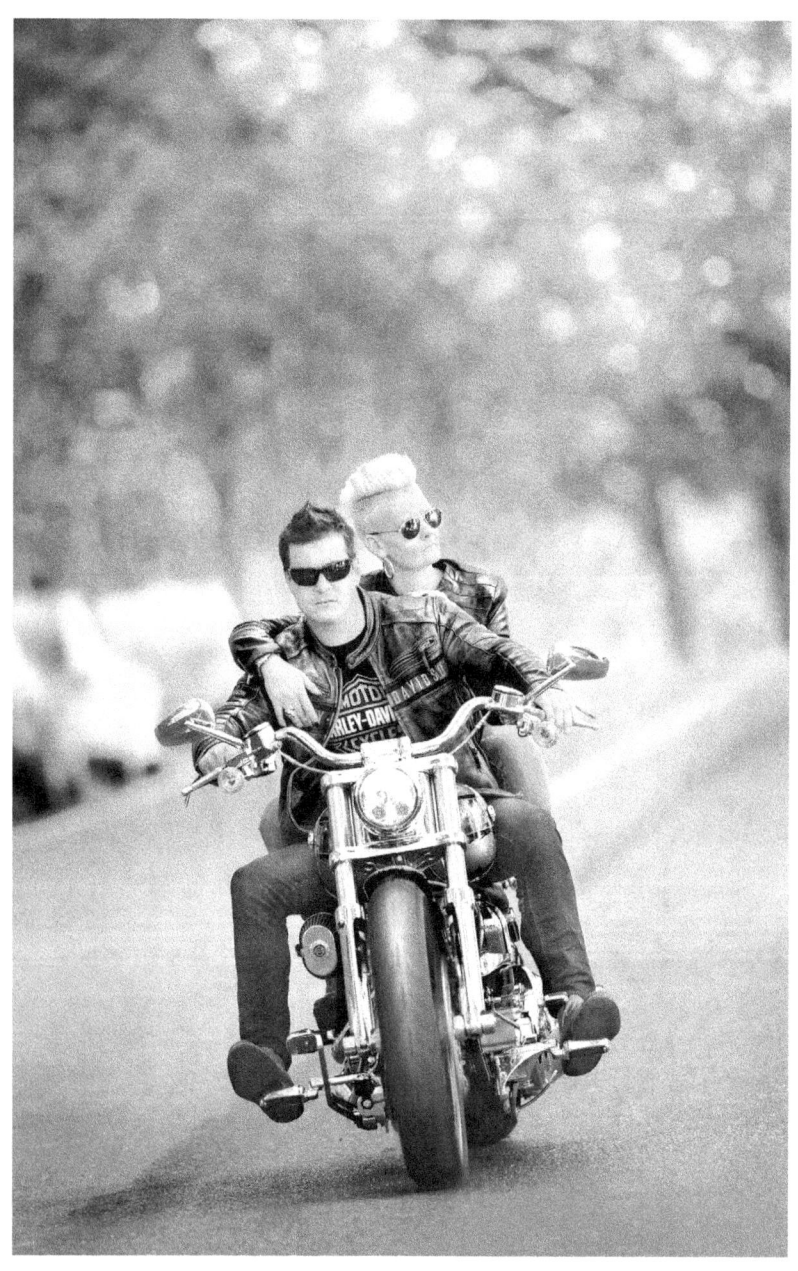

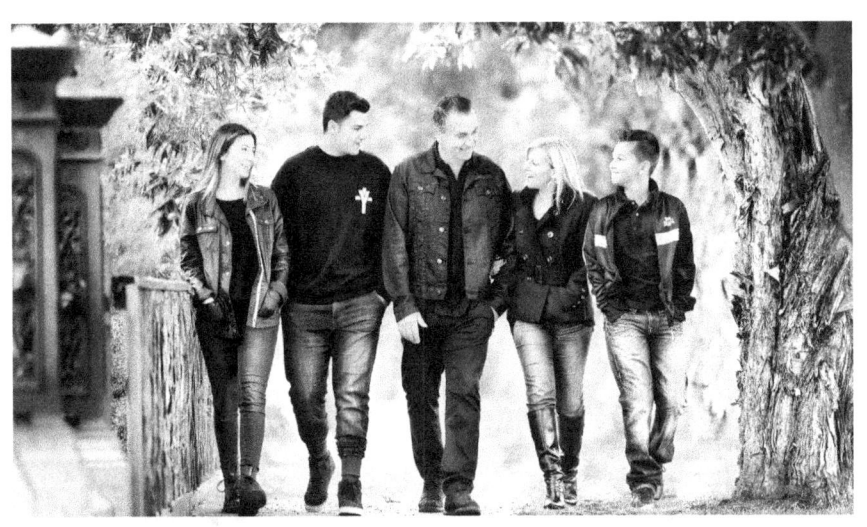

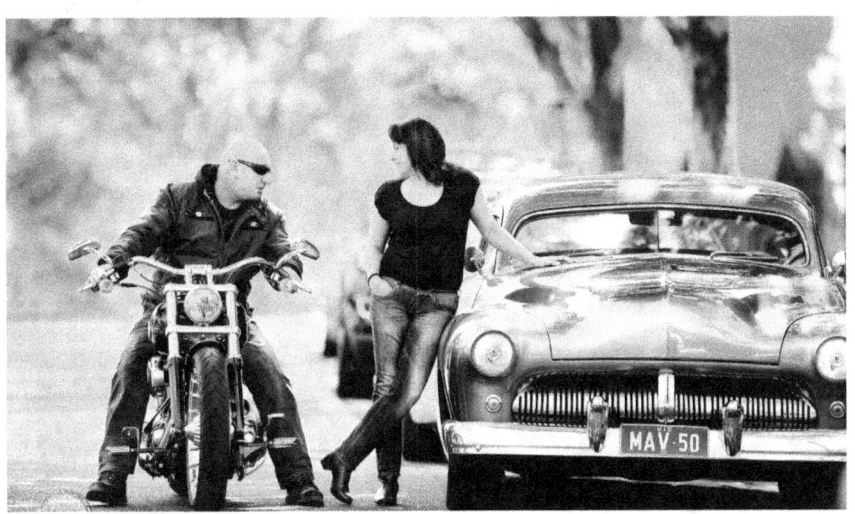

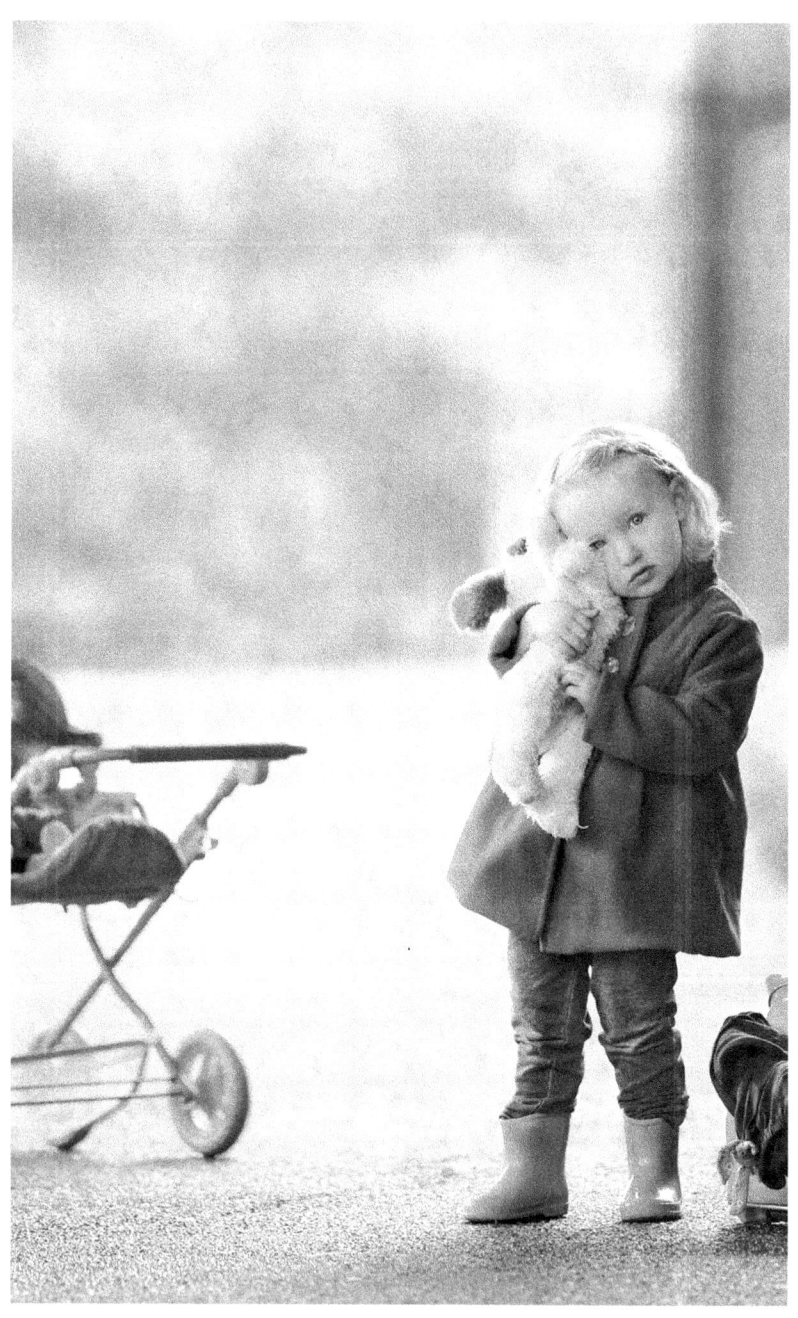

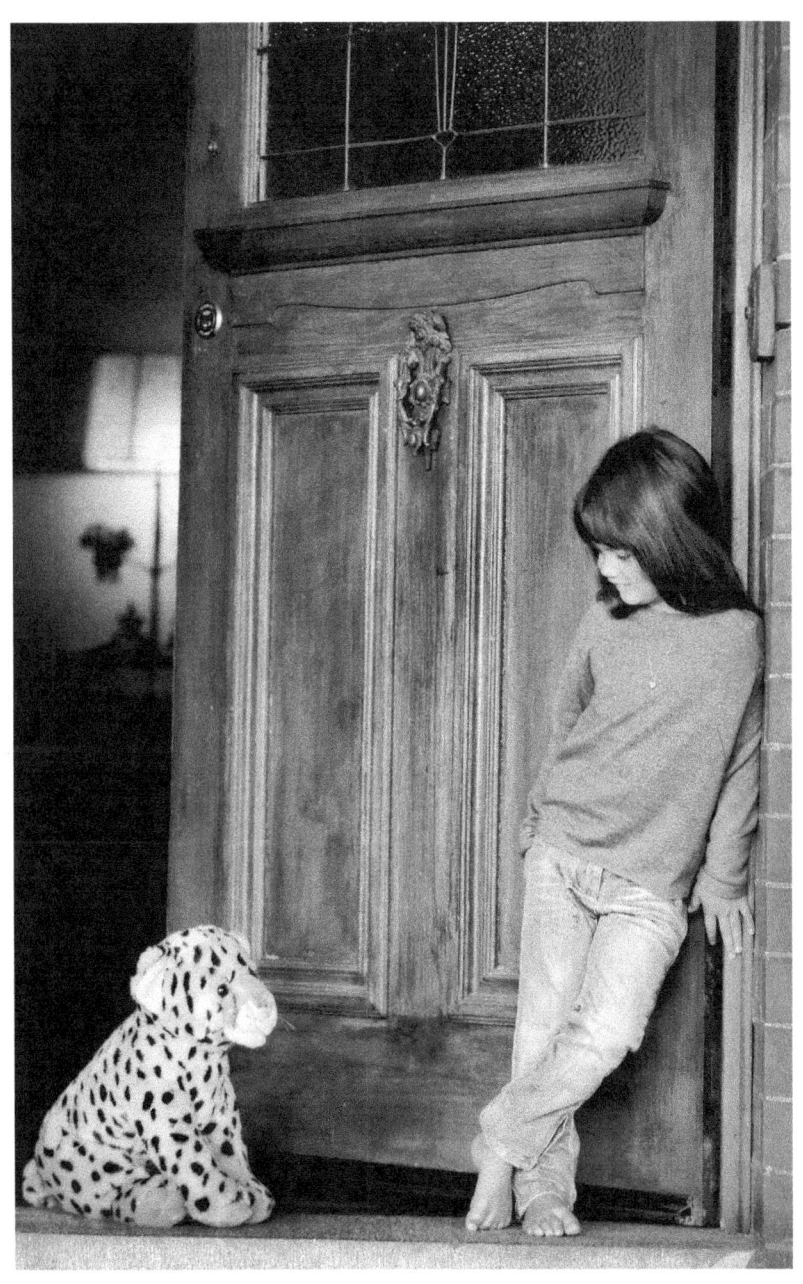

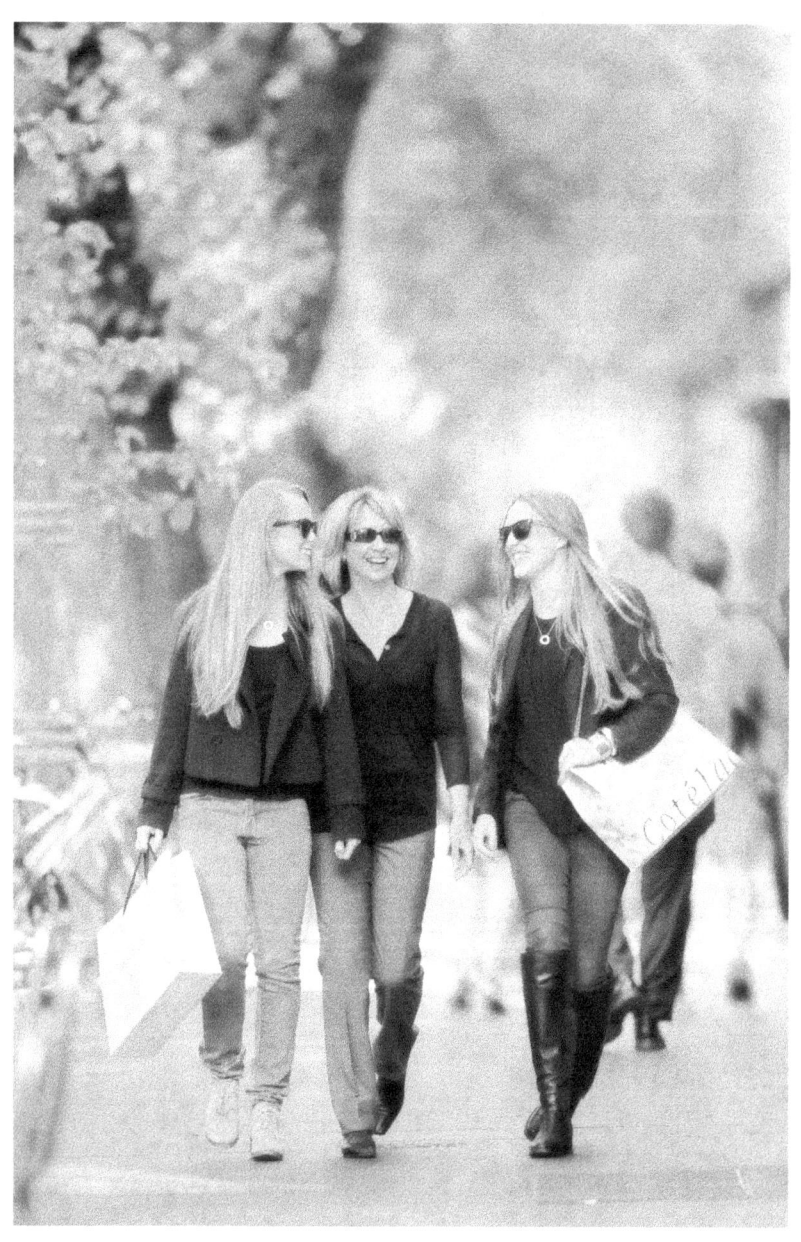

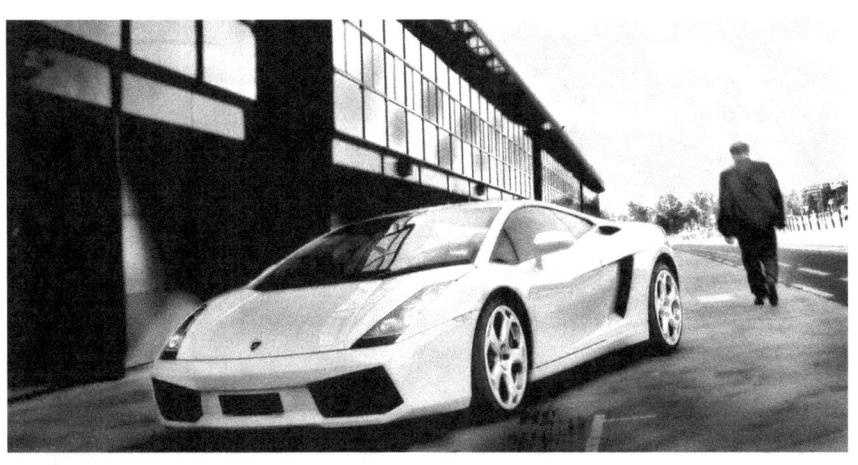

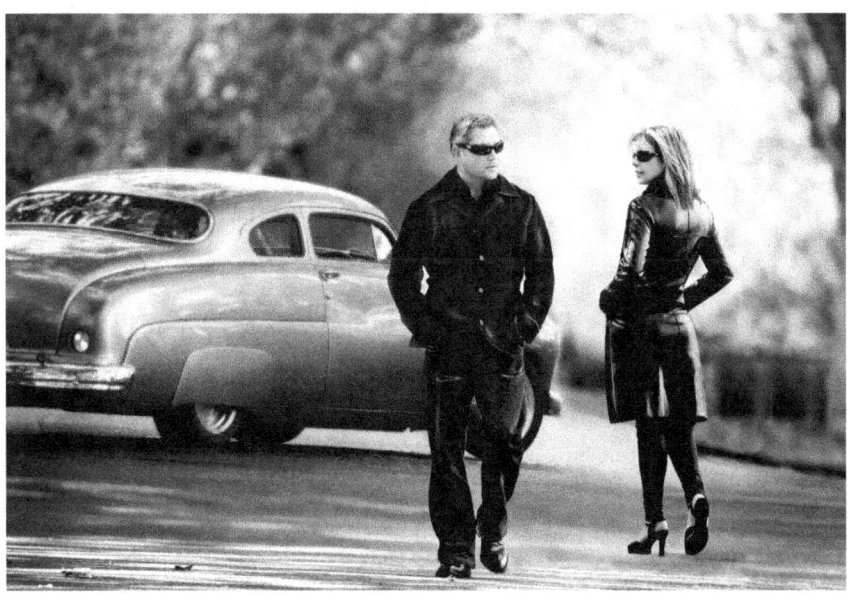

ACKNOWLEDGEMENTS

A special thanks to everyone that
helped make this book.

Firstly I want to acknowledge my wife Tracey Tilnak for supporting me through this first book in understanding how much it means for me to share my knowledge. Also Kathleen Rebecca Tilnak, my daughter who believes in me and is probably my biggest fan. Finally, my circle of friends who have shown a renewed interest in their photography and this book.

Editors:

Linda Broadbent (PhD) Lindy as her friends call her is an incredible woman. She is one of these people that has a vast knowledge in so many different areas. Thank you, Lindy, for the editing and feedback along this journey.

Tanya Lee: A school teacher by profession. A photographer in her own right, she is presently my number one assistant on 'Lifestyle Portraits' photographic shoots. Her meticulous attention to detail is second to none, and I much appreciate and thank you for doing the final edit.

Photographers:

Front cover: Peter Casamento from Casamento photography.

Peter, is a long-standing commercial photographer with over 23 years experience professionally. The front cover that he created is striking and I feel honoured that he portrayed me in this way.

Back cover: Luke Myers from Luke Myers photography.

Luke is an actor and professional photographer, specialising in head shots. His communication and vision is superior and he makes you feel very special when he photographs you. Luke my friend, thank you for everything.

I would like to leave you with a quote that rings so true to me:
"Amateurs worry about equipment,
Professionals worry about time and
Masters worry about light" ~ Unknown author

Adege	Kei Scampa
Alexas_Fotos	Keith JJ
Anastacia Knits	KoalaPark Laundromat
Cindy Gustafson	LoboStudio Hamburg
Dariusz Sankowski	Mateus Campos Felipe
Davidsonluna	Max Fischer
Dibakar Roy	Mehrsa Saberi
Ferenc Horvath	Nuno Antunes
Fikret Kabay	Peter Fazekas
FotoshopTofs	Peter Fischer
Foundry	Ryan Hafey
Gantas Vaičiulėnas	Sergey Pesterev
Gui Avelar	Sharegrid
Helena Lopes	Stefano Zocca
Hello I'm Nik	Stock Snap
Ibrahim Boran	Taryn Elliot
Josh Hild	World Spectrum
Juraj Masar	Wynand Van Poortvliet

They say an image is worth a thousand words and so it was important to insert images that helped tell the story throughout this book. Because I am a specialist in the portrait area, I felt it is important to inject other forms of photography and genres. Therefore, I sourced images from the public domain that helped explain each subsection of the chapter where applicable. I would like to acknowledge each and every photographer who generously shares their photography on the public domain through websites like Unsplash, Pixabay and Pexels. "Photographers, I salute you." The names of the photographers are listed above.

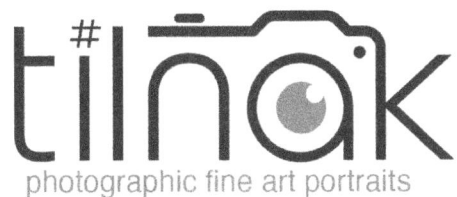

photographic fine art portraits

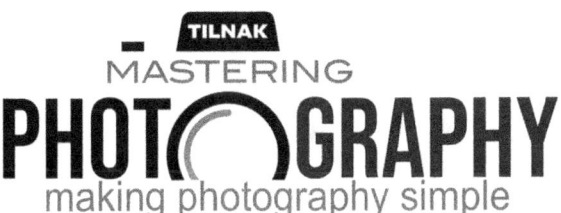

making photography simple

www.ingramcontent.com/pod-product-compliance
Lightning Source LLC
Chambersburg PA
CBHW071206220526
45468CB00002B/513